Jacqueline Briggs Martin and YOU

**Recent titles in
The Author and YOU Series**
Sharron McElmeel, Series Editor

Gerald McDermott and YOU
Jon C. Stott, Foreword and Illustrations by Gerald McDermott

Alma Flor Ada and YOU, Volume I
Alma Flor Ada

Jim Aylesworth and YOU
Jim Aylesworth and Jennifer K. Rotole

Toni Buzzeo and YOU
Toni Buzzeo

Jacqueline Briggs Martin and YOU

Jacqueline Briggs Martin
with Sharron L. McElmeel

The Author and YOU

Sharron McElmeel, Series Editor

Westport, Connecticut • London

Library of Congress Cataloging-in-Publication Data

Martin, Jacqueline Briggs.
   Jacqueline Briggs Martin and you / by Jacqueline Briggs Martin with Sharron L. McElmeel.
      p. cm.—(The author and you)
   Includes bibliographical references and index.
   ISBN 1-59158-257-1 (pbk. : alk. paper)
      1. Martin, Jacqueline Briggs. 2. Authors, American—20th century—Biography.
3. Children's stories—Authorship. 4. Reading promotion. 5. Illustration of books.
I. McElmeel, Sharron L. II. Title. III. Series.
PS3563.A7242Z76   2006
813'.54—dc22   2005030802

British Library Cataloguing in Publication Data is available.

Copyright © 2006 by Jacqueline Briggs Martin

All rights reserved. No portion of this book may be
reproduced, by any process or technique, without the
express written consent of the publisher.

Library of Congress Catalog Card Number: 2005030802
ISBN: 1-59158-257-1

First published in 2006

Libraries Unlimited, 88 Post Road West, Westport, CT 06881
A Member of the Greenwood Publishing Group, Inc.
www.lu.com

The paper used in this book complies with the
Permanent Paper Standard issued by the National
Information Standards Organization (Z39.48–1984).

10 9 8 7 6 5 4 3 2 1

To readers, writers, and story lovers—all ages, all sizes
J.B.M.

Contents

Series Foreword   xi
Sharon Coatney
Sharron L. McElmeel

Introduction   xiii
Sharron L. McElmeel

PART I

A Writer's Path—from Maine to Iowa   3
Sharron L. McElmeel

Frequently Asked Questions   11

Jacqueline Briggs Martin's Bookshelf   13
  Banjo Granny's Song   13
  Bizzy Bones Series   13
  Button, Bucket, Sky   14
  Chicken Joy on Redbean Road   14
  The Finest Horse in Town   14
  Good Times on Grandfather Mountain   14
  Grandmother Bryant's Pocket   15
  Green Truck Garden Giveaway: A Neighborhood Story
    and Almanac   16
  Higgins Bend Song and Dance   16
  The Lamp, the Ice, and the Boat Called *Fish*   16
  On Sand Island   17
  Snowflake Bentley   17
  Washing the Willow Tree Loon   18
  The Water Gift and the Pig of the Pig   18

Notes about the Artists   19
  Azarian, Mary   19
  Carpenter, Nancy   20
  Gaber, Susan   20
  Gillman, Alec   21
  Johnson, David A.   21
  Krommes, Beth   21
  Mathers, Petra   22
  Ormai, Stella   22
  Redenbaugh, Vicki Jo   23
  Root, Barry   23
  Sneed, Brad   23
  Sweet, Melissa   24
  Wingerter, Linda S.   24

PART II

An Author's Letter to YOU! 29

Why Write? 31
    Filling the Room We Call Our Imagination 33
    Books: The Best Writing Teachers 34

Writing: Work or Play? When to Write? What to Write? 35
    Writing as Play, Writing for Fun 35
    Writing as Work 36
    When to Write 36
    What to Write: Where do I Find Ideas for Writing? 37

Writing Longer Pieces 39
    Writing about a Favorite Place 39
    A Sampling: Books about Place 43
    Writing about a Person 44
        Writing about My "Hero" 44
    A Sampling: Books about People 46
    Writing a Family Story 47
        Writing My Family Story 47
    A Sampling: Family Stories in Books 50

Nonfiction 53
    Research for *The Lamp, the Ice, and the Boat Called* Fish 53
    Writing the Story 54

Writing a Made-up Story 57
    A Made-up Story in a Historical Time: *Grandmother Bryant's Pocket* 57
    Wonderful Surprises 59
    Inventing the Characters for Made-up Stories 59
    Finding Story Ideas for Made-up Stories 59
        Ideas from What We Love to Do 60
        Ideas from Reading 60
        Ideas from Elevators, Buses, and Sidewalks 61

PART III

Writer's Notebook 65
    A Writer's Notebook—For All Those Who Seek to Be a Writer 65
        Journals 65
    A Selected Booklist—Journaling 65
        Books about Journaling 65
        Picture Books Written in Journal Format 65

Some Fiction and Nonfiction Books for Older Readers Written
   in Journal or Letter Format   66
Getting Started   66
   Finding the Tools   66
   Making an Accordion Notebook   67
   Making a Two-holed Notebook   68
   Folded Mini Notebook   69
Finding the Writing Tools   70
Filling Those Pages   71
   1. Letters   71
   2. Jokes and Riddles   73
   3. Recipes   74
   *Some Picture Books (Including a Couple of Tall Tales) about Food,
      Recipes to Give You Ideas for Recipe Stories*   75
   4. How-to   76
   How to Make Your Own Bubble Mix   76
   5. Details   77
   6. What If?   77
Writing Longer Pieces: Writing about a Favorite Place   78
Writing Longer Pieces: Writing about Your Hero   79
   Learning about the Person   80
   Doing the Writing   80
   Writing a Family Story   81
   Finding the Topic   81
   Beginning to Write   81
   Shaping the Story   82
   Nonfiction: Finding a Nonfiction Story that Interests You   82
   Doing the Research   85
   Who? What? Where? When? Why?   85
   Finding Answers: Starting at Home   86
   A Local Resource   86
   Going to the Library   87
   Internet   87
   How Do You Know When You Know Enough? When Do We Quit
      Researching?   87
   Telling the Story   87

Writing YOUR Made-up Story   89
   Where Will You Get Ideas?   89
      Ideas from Our Own Lives   89
      Ideas from What We Love to Do   89
      Ideas from Reading   89
      Listening and Watching for Ideas   90

Oh No, No Ideas! 90
Go to Your Journal 90
A Real Event 90
Piggyback Stories 91
Tall Tales 91
After You Get the Idea, What Next? 92
Questions 92
Some Possible Story Shapes 93
Stories about Problems 93
When the Character Is the Problem 94
Journey Problems 94
Descriptive Stories 95
Who Is Telling the Story? 95
Revising 96
What Next? 97
What Will You Do with Your Writing 97
A Reading for Friends and Family 97
Self-publishing Your Story 99
Publishing Your Story in a Magazine 99
The Room with Beautiful Windows 100

For More Information about the Author and Other Resources 101

Articles 101
Websites 101

Photo Credits 103

Index 105

Series Foreword

Have you ever wanted to sit down and talk with the author of a beloved story? Have you ever wanted to find out more? Good authors are like good friends. They touch our hearts and minds. They make us wonder, and want to learn.

When young readers become engaged with a story, they invariably ask questions.

- Why is Gerald McDermott so fascinated with myths and legends? How did he locate and choose which stories he wished to retell? How do the images in his books convey the culture represented in the story while still retaining his own artistic vision?
- Did Alma Flor Ada know the people that we meet in her stories? Where does she come from? Why does she write in Spanish and English?
- Can Toni Buzzeo tell us how much of *The Sea Chest* is legend and what part is fact? What character does she like best: the Dawdle Ducking, Papa Loon? How does she get her ideas?

As teachers and librarians, we know that the moment children begin asking questions, we are presented with a wonderful opportunity. In response, we may hold discussions or create learning activities. Yet, answers to some questions are hard to come by. After all, our students and we cannot just sit down and talk with the authors we love and admire. But wouldn't it be great if we could?

Libraries Unlimited has developed *The Author and YOU* series to give you the next best thing to a real-life visit with your favorite children's authors and illustrators. In these books, you'll hear from authors and illustrators as they reflect on their work and explain to YOU, the reader, what they really had in mind. You'll find answers to some of the questions you and your students might ask and to some you never thought to ask.

Just as each author or illustrator is a unique individual, so will his or her conversation with YOU be unique and individual. There is no formula, no predesigned structure. We've simply asked the authors or illustrators to discuss the things they each think are important or interesting about themselves and their books—and to share their comments with YOU.

Some authors will provide actual ideas and plans for you to use in sharing books with young readers. Others will share ideas that will help you generate your own ideas and connections to their work. In some cases the author writes the book in collaboration with another. In others, it is a private reflection; but in all cases you'll discover some fascinating information and come away with valuable insights.

It is our hope that by giving you these special messages from authors and illustrators, *The Author and YOU* series will increase your joy and understanding of literature—and in turn, will help YOU motivate young readers, surround them with literacy and literacy activities, and share the joy of understanding.

Sharon Coatney
Sharron McElmeel

Introduction

I am thrilled that Jacqueline Briggs Martin is now added to the list of prestigious and talented authors and illustrators featured in Libraries Unlimited's Author and YOU series. I first became acquainted when a librarian who was enrolled in a course I was teaching proudly announced that the small town she was from was the home to a wonderful author. She brought in the "wonderful author's" books and talked at length about this author who she was sure would have many more books published. That author was Jacqueline Briggs Martin. My first autographed book signed by Jacqueline is dated 1987. At that time she had two books published. Years later there are many of her books on my bookshelves and she has become a popular author of picture books, and she has become my friend. Her 1998 title, *Snowflake Bentley*, was illustrated by Mary Azarian, who was given the prestigious Caldecott Award for her magnificent illustrations for this book. As a native of Maine, Jacqueline has earned the state's Lupine Award three times. The Lupine Award has honored: *Grandmother Bryant's Pocket*, *Snowflake Bentley*, and *The Water Gift and the Pig of the Pig*.

Her writing has been called lyrical, poetic, and magnificent prose. She is able to describe her characters with phrases so wonderful we know exactly the types of persons they are. Her books are populated with scientists, explorers, grandfathers with the water gift, eternal optimists—Old Washburn, a fisherman who is determined to catch the wily catfish Oscar, and a villain who was so mean he "wouldn't give away the good smell from a piece of warm toast." Her books are filled with information about people and places. They take us to the eighteenth century, to the northernmost area of Alaska, to a small town in Maine, and to the river to go fishing.

In this book she speaks of one of her passions—the art of writing. She encourages families to read together and to write some of their stories. She nurtures writers and promotes reading. Throughout this book she shares how she uses her own quest for information to fuel her writing. She talks of how reading provides her with answers to her questions and stimulates more questions. She invites you the reader—young or old—to join her, to read and write with her.

Sharron L. McElmeel
www.mcelmeel.com

A Writer's Path—from Maine to Iowa

An Introduction by Sharron L. McElmeel

Jacqueline's mother, Alice, as a young girl growing up in Maine.

Although Jacqueline Briggs Martin may not have realized it at the time, she began collecting bits and pieces for her writing during her growing up years in Maine and later in Iowa as a wife, mother, and preschool teacher. Jacqueline was born in Lewiston, Maine on April 15 shortly after World War II ended. Her childhood was spent on the family farm. Her parents, Hugh and Alice Briggs, operated a dairy farm. Alice's mother, Cora (Jacqueline's grandmother), had died shortly after the birth of Alice's twin brother and sister so Alice had grown up helping to care for her brother and sister.

Jacqueline's father, Hugh, and her grandfather on the family farm. Jacqueline's father is on the right.

The farm Jacqueline grew up on has been in the family for seven generations. Her father tended the meadow and worked the land. Her mother was bookkeeper for the family farm. Together Jacqueline's parents raised six children—Jacqueline and her two sisters and three brothers.

The Briggs's Family Farm near Lewiston, Maine.

Jacqueline Briggs Martin (circa: 1948).

Jacqueline and her two sisters; L to R: Laura, Jacqueline, Audrey.

Jacqueline's three brothers; L to R: David, Hugh, Stephen.

The family named the cows and each had a name referring to the bloodline and place of birth. One of the cows, Blanche Wisconsin, later found her way into one of Jacqueline's books, *Good Times on Grandfather Mountain*.

Every day, while riding the bus to school, Jacqueline rode past her cousin's apple orchard. The apples were often used in pies and other baked goods. Jacqueline remembers one day, for a special event, when her mother and a few of her mother's friends made fifty apple pies. Jacqueline also remembers the beautiful quilts her mother pieced together for many family members and for friends.

When Jacqueline and her siblings were young, Jacqueline and one of her brothers tried to rescue injured birds. The two of them did not have much success, but the memories of their efforts stayed with her. Years later she wrote

During school visits Jacqueline Briggs Martin sometimes shares a picture of Blanche Wisconsin, a cow whose name she used in *Good Times on Grandfather Mountain* (circa. 1992).

Photo credit: Sharron L. McElmeel

about rescuing a loon, *Washing the Willow Tree Loon*. She researched successful rescue programs, and this time, in her book, her characters were successful in saving the bird.

Jacqueline's childhood gave her many memories. She sometimes took short road trips in the cab of a big cattle truck driven by an uncle. She loved listening to her uncle sing of "rovers and riverboat riders." That song became part of *Bizzy Bones and Moosemouse*. Her family lived in the upper part of the large home on the family farm. Jacqueline's grandparents lived in the lower level surrounding her with family, words, stories, and a variety of rich experiences.

Jacqueline grew up and earned a graduate degree in child development from the University of Minnesota. During her college years, while traveling back home to Maine, Jacqueline met her future husband, Richard Martin. She and Richard first lived in Chicago and later moved to Mount Vernon, Iowa, where together they raised two children, Sarah and Justin. Richard Martin is a professor in the English department at Cornell College, a small Midwestern college nestled on a sprawling campus in a picturesque Iowa small town.

Jacqueline wrote occasionally during her high school and college days, but later, as she embarked on her career as a preschool teacher and began to raise her family, she put aside her writing. When Sarah was born, Jacqueline began reading daily to her and the reading sessions continued when Justin was born. Jacqueline read many picture books. She

fell in love with picture books and the desire to write returned. She began to write stories—stories that might become picture books. Jacqueline wrote while her children napped and when they gave up naps she got up at 4 A.M. in order to have writing time.

She wrote for several years before her first book, *Bizzy Bones and Uncle Ezra*, was published in 1984. The story, *Bizzy Bones and Uncle Ezra*, grew out of her son Justin's fear of the wind. At first the story featured a small boy and his parents, but as Jacqueline wrote and rewrote the story the boy became a small mouse, Bizzy Bones, and the parents were replaced by Uncle Ezra. Uncle Ezra was named for one of the family's favorite authors at the time, Ezra Jack Keats. Bizzy Bones is a young mouse that is afraid of the wind. Uncle Ezra builds a carousel that uses the scary wind to make a good ride.

Jacqueline and her children shared many stories and books over the years. When they read a magazine article about Wilson A. Bentley they remembered him, and while walking through fresh Iowa snow one of the children might comment that the day was one Snowflake Bentley would have surely liked. Eventually Sarah and Justin suggested to their mom

Mary Azarian (1999)   Jacqueline Briggs Martin (1999)

Azarian and Martin signing their Caldecott Award Winning book, *Snowflake Bentley* during the American Library Association's annual convention in New Orleans, LA.

Photo credit: Sharron L. McElmeel

that she write about Snowflake Bentley. When her story was finished, the publisher asked Mary Azarian to illustrate the book. Azarian is a gifted woodcut artist. The pictures she created for *Snowflake Bentley* earned her the 1999 Randolph Caldecott Award for outstanding illustrations. While the award is given to the illustrator, the text of the winning book must be "worthy of the illustrations." Jacqueline's and Mary Azarian's joint efforts created an outstanding biography about an interesting person who came to be known across the United States (and even in China and Japan through editions translated into those languages).

The apple orchard she rode past on the school bus and the stone fences in the fields where she often walked during her childhood became part of the *Bizzy Bones* books and also played a role in a book about her aunts, *The Finest Horse in Town*.

Jacqueline loves writing, but she says, "I can't write all day. When I'm not writing I read, or walk outside, or do all the things we all have to do—cook, wash dishes, sweep the floors." She also bakes bread. She and a couple of friends regularly meet in Jacqueline's spacious kitchen to bake bread—two or three times a week. They supply the bread for a local restaurant market and use the profits to support environmental and humanitarian projects. "Olive's Sisters" choose different causes to contribute to, depending on what is going on in their community at the time.

Like her mother, Jacqueline also likes to make quilts—but only "if I am doing it with someone I love." In *Bizzy Bones and the Lost Quilt*, Stella Ormai used the images of a few of Jacqueline's mother's quilts as rugs hanging on the Orchard Mice's clothesline.

In the warm seasons Jacqueline enjoys working outside. She grows roses, chillies, and herbs for tomato sauce. When her daughter, Sarah, was an elementary student, a friend helped Sarah plant a prairie garden based on Sarah's favorite books at the time, the Laura Ingalls Wilder's Little House series.

Jacqueline still tends that garden. She also enjoys tent camping, hiking, and canoeing, watching rivers, and watching fish.

Sarah Martin at the age she planted the Laura Ingalls Wilder garden.

Jacqueline in her rose garden. Circa. 2003

As you read the books authored by Jacqueline Briggs Martin you will find pieces of her life in each of her books.

Today she and her husband Rich live in Mt. Vernon, Iowa and travel often to Maine, Massachusetts, Indiana, Ohio, and Wisconsin to visit family.

Frequently Asked Questions

Q. When did you first start writing?
A. When Sarah was in preschool and Justin was a baby.
Q. How did you get your first book published?
A. I had written a story about a witch and sent it off to a publisher. The publisher did not want a book about witches but offered to look at any other stories I might have. When I finished a new story about a little mouse that was afraid of the wind, I sent it back to the same publisher. They liked the story and eventually offered to publish the book. That book was my first and was called *Bizzy Bones and Uncle Ezra*.
Q. What kind of writing schedule do you keep now that you are a "full-time" writer?
A. I like writing in the morning. If I am doing research I can do research in the afternoon, but I rarely write in the afternoon. I try to write every day and often can do that except when I am traveling.
Q. Do you like to write?
A. I love the sounds of words and love making up stories. I also love to read and find out new things. Through my writing, I can share interesting stories of real people and real events.

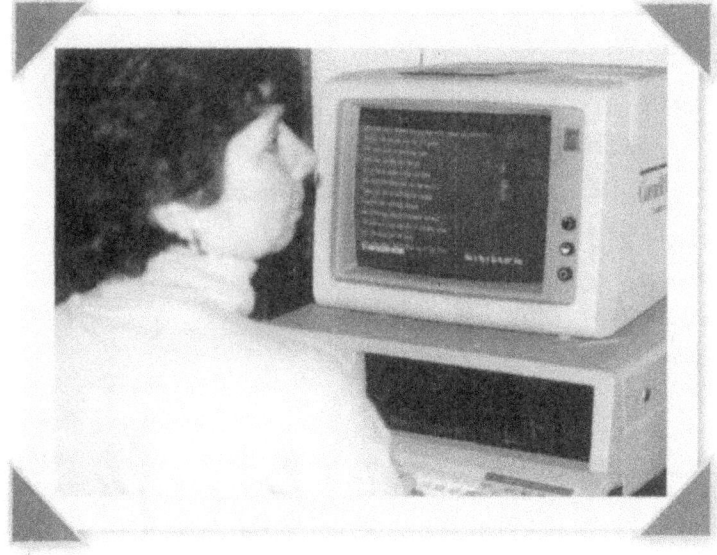

Jacqueline writes firstdrafts in a tablet or notebook but transfers her stories to her computer for editing and rewriting.

Photo credit:
Sharron L. McElmeel

Q. How long does it take you to write a book?
A. Many of my stories require months of research. It takes additional months to actually write the story. One of my books, *Bizzy Bones and the Lost Quilt*, took only one and one-half years from the time I got the story idea to having the published book in my hands. Some of my books have taken up to four years.
Q. Do you illustrate your own books?
A. No, the publisher chooses the artists for my books. So far, a number of very talented artists have created the illustrations for my books. Stella Ormai illustrated the first three of my books and later books were illustrated by: Brad Sneed, Mary Azarian, Susan Gaber, Linda S. Wingerter, Beth Krommes, Vicki Jo Redenbaugh, Nancy Carpenter, Petra Mathers, Alec Gillman, David A. Johnson, Barry Root, and Melissa Sweet.
Q. When you read to your children, what were your favorite books to read to them?
A. The Curious George stories, some Dr. Seuss stories (especially *One Fish, Two Fish, Red Fish, Blue Fish* and *The Five Hundred Hats of Bartholomew Cubbins*), *Chicken Soup with Rice*, the *Babar the Elephant* series, and *Louie*, by Ezra Jack Keats. At the time I was writing the Bizzy Bones books we especially loved the books by Ezra Jack Keats. Bizzy Bones's uncle was named Ezra in his honor.

Jacqueline Briggs Martin's Bookshelf

BANJO GRANNY'S SONG

Banjo Granny's Song. Co-authored with Sarah Martin Busse. Illustrated by Barry Root. (Houghton, 2006.)

A tale of a granny who misses her faraway grandchild so much that she puts on her thousand-mile shoes and, to the rhythm of a bluegrass tune, makes her way across the prairies and mountains to reach the grandchild she longs to see.

BIZZY BONES SERIES

Bizzy Bones Series—Each of these books is about Bizzy Bones, a little mouse who lives with his beloved Uncle Ezra. All of the books are illustrated by Stella Ormai.

Bizzy Bones and Moosemouse (Lothrop, 1986).
Bizzy is apprehensive about staying the weekend with Uncle Ezra's friend Moosemouse.

Bizzy Bones and the Lost Quilt (Lothrop, 1988).
Bizzy Bones loses his favorite quilt, but with the help of friends his quilt, although tattered, is found and repaired with a large apple tree patch.

Bizzy Bones and Uncle Ezra (Lothrop, 1984).
Uncle Ezra helps Bizzy Bones overcome his fear of the wind.

BUTTON, BUCKET, SKY

Button, Bucket, Sky. Illustrated by Vicki Jo Redenbaugh. (Carolrhoda, 1998.)

Facts about planting acorns and growing oak trees are central to this story about young naturalists who plant their own trees.

CHICKEN JOY ON REDBEAN ROAD

Chicken Joy on Redbean Road. Illustrated by Melissa Sweet. (Houghton Mifflin, 2007.)

Set in Cajun country in Louisiana this tale features a blue-headed rooster who loses his voice after a case of the chicken measles. He is in danger of becoming "quiet rooster stew" until his friend, a plain brown hen who calls herself Cleoma, brings in musicians to inspire him to return to his singing (crowing) and avoid the stew pot. *Chicken Joy on Redbean Road* is a literary tall tale about friendship in the chicken yard and the healing power of Louisiana music.

THE FINEST HORSE IN TOWN

The Finest Horse in Town. Illustrated by Susan Gaber. (HarperCollins, 1992; Purple House Press, 2003.)

This book results from the author's curiosity about the lives of her two great-aunts who operated a dry-goods store and had "the finest horse in town." Martin imagines three situations concerning who cares for the horse, Prince, while his owners, the author's two great-aunts, are operating their dry-goods store. NOTE—Look for the stone walls and the apple trees.

GOOD TIMES ON GRANDFATHER MOUNTAIN

Good Times on Grandfather Mountain. Illustrated by Susan Gaber. (Orchard, 1992.)

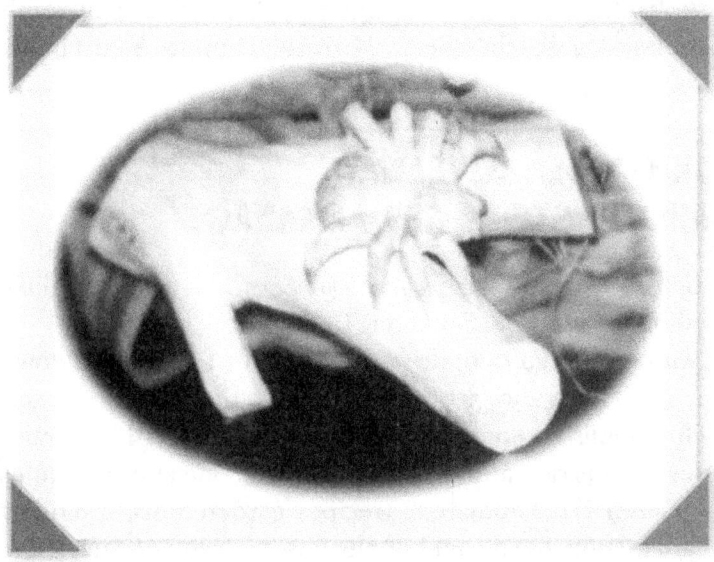

A spider from a stick similar to one that Old Washburn whittled in *Good Times on Grandfather Mountain*.

Photo credit: Sharron L. McElmeel

Continually optimistic, Old Washburn lives on the mountain with his animals. He is able to retain his positive attitude even as his animals leave his mountain home, one by one. He makes music and whittles a fiddle from his fallen-down house and a spider from a stick.

When Old Washburn's neighbors hear the fiddle music, they come for dancing and carpentering. The animals return to join into the festivities.

GRANDMOTHER BRYANT'S POCKET

Grandmother Bryant's Pocket. Illustrated by Petra Mathers. (Houghton Mifflin, 1996.)

After Sarah's dog, Patches, is caught in a fire, she has dreams that won't be calmed. Her parents send her to live with her grandmother and grandfather Bryant. Grandmother Bryant is a healer and Grandfather Bryant a whittler. In the late 1700s, women's outer garments did not have pockets. Women often wore, under their skirts, an apron-like garment that did have a pocket. A slit in the side of their skirt allowed them to reach into their pocket. Grandmother Bryant's pocket contained her most

important possessions. It was her grandmother's pocket that helped Sarah deal with the loss of her dog, Patches. Set in 1787. 1996 Lupine Award book.

GREEN TRUCK GARDEN GIVEAWAY: A NEIGHBORHOOD STORY AND ALMANAC

Green Truck Garden Giveaway: A Neighborhood Story and Almanac. Illustrated by Alec Gillman. (Simon & Schuster, 1997.)

Two friends, who love to garden, drive their green truck up and down the streets of their small town and give away gardens to their neighbors and in the process help establish a community of friends. The neighbors raise tomatoes and herbs and berries, and begin to share with one another. Notes from the friends' "Green Truck Almanac" (recipes, garden hints, and other interesting facts) are included in a panel on the lower portion of each page.

HIGGINS BEND SONG AND DANCE

Higgins Bend Song and Dance. Illustrated by Brad Sneed. (Houghton Mifflin, 1997.)

Simon Henry used to go fishing with his friend Potato Kelly, until "too much work and tight boots" bring on a grouchy spell. His friend Potato Kelly, who owns the bait and chowder shop near Higgins Bend, bets Simon Henry that he cannot catch the wily catfish, Oscar. When Oscar steals Simon Henry's doughballs, his fat redworms, and his best five-day-old secret recipe stinkbait, the contest is on and Simon Henry vows "to get up early, work late, and sleep in my boots" until that fish is caught. If you like fishing, like rivers, or just like to laugh, you will like this story.

THE LAMP, THE ICE, AND THE BOAT CALLED *FISH*

The Lamp, the Ice, and the Boat Called Fish. Illustrated by Beth Krommes. (Houghton Mifflin, 2001.)

A dramatic tale of the last voyage of the *Karluk*. The *Karluk*, part of an expedition led by Arctic explorer Vilhjalmur Stefansson, became icebound. Stefansson left the ship and many crew members and scientists. This story tells how these crew members and scientists managed to survive for months with the help of an Iñupiaq family, aboard to help sew and hunt. Based on a true story.

ON SAND ISLAND

On Sand Island. Illustrated by David A. Johnson. (Houghton Mifflin, 2003.)

Living on an island in Lake Superior, in the early twentieth century, Carl dreams of having a boat of his own. With ingenuity, help from his neighbors, and hard work he manages to build himself a small boat. Glorious watercolors.

SNOWFLAKE BENTLEY

Snowflake Bentley. Illustrated by Mary Azarian. (Houghton, 1998.)

Caldecott Award Book (1999). A narrative biography of Wilson A. Bentley who lived in Jericho, Vermont in the late nineteenth century and early twentieth century. Sidebars fill in the gaps with statistics and additional information about Bentley and his love of snow. 1998 Lupine Award book.

WASHING THE WILLOW TREE LOON

Washing the Willow Tree Loon. Illustrated by Nancy Carpenter. (Simon & Schuster, 1995.)

An oil-soaked loon is rescued from an oil spill in fictional Turtle Bay. Many people who are involved in rescuing the loon are profiled as they work to save the bird. A two-page author's note provides additional information about bird rescue.

THE WATER GIFT AND THE PIG OF THE PIG

The Water Gift and the Pig of the Pig. Illustrated by Linda S. Wingerter. (Houghton Mifflin, 2003.)

Winner of the 2003 Lupine Award, this book is set on the coast of Maine. Isabel's grandfather has the water gift—he can detect water with a divining rod. Isabel is quiet and shy and her best friend is the Pig of the Pig. When her grandfather listens to one too many neighbors and loses faith in himself and the pig of the pig wanders away, it is Isabel who figures out what to do.

Notes about the Artists

While the author writes the text for a picture book. An artist's role is to interpret the story, to research appropriate images, and to help bring two art forms together, literature and visual art. Once the author submits the manuscript to a publisher and it is accepted for publication, an editor works with the author and then an art editor selects an artist to create the illustrations. Most often the author and the illustrator never meet—or at least do not meet until the book is completed. It is the art editor who provides the guidance to the artist. The text editor and art editor work together to give the author and the illustrator freedom to be creative in their own way. Sometimes the artist causes some changes in the text; for example, if an artist can show in a picture something that is in the text, that phrase or sentence might be eliminated from the text. The author would make that change if he/she agrees. Despite the fact that an award might go specifically to the author for the text or to the illustrator for the illustrations, one must recognize that unless the other element is also well done the book, as a whole, would probably not be considered for the award. In fact, Mary Azarian was honored for her illustrations for Jacqueline Briggs Martin's *Snowflake Bentley*—and although the honor was given specifically for the illustrations, the criteria for the award states: "The committee is to make its decision primarily on the illustrations, but other components of a book are to be considered especially when they make a book less effective as a children's picture book. Such other components might include the written text, the overall design of the book, etc." Illustrations do make a difference to the text, and the text provides the foundation for the illustrations. Jacqueline Briggs Martin has been fortunate that the art editors working on her books have selected some very talented artists to illustrate her texts.

Azarian, Mary

Mary Azarian was born in 1940 in Washington, D.C. She studied painting and printmaking at Smith College. After her graduation, in 1963, she and her partner/husband moved to Vermont where the two of them raised three sons and kept horses, oxen, chickens, a milk cow, and sheep. They also made maple syrup and kept a large vegetable and flower garden. By 1969 she had also established Farmhouse Press and began producing woodcut prints. At first she printed the woodcuts by hand and eventually began using a nineteenth-century Vandercook proof press. Her early prints were black and white and eventually she perfected a technique to add color using water-based paints. While other woodcut artists most often add color with an additional color block for printing, Azarian continues to hand-color her prints, making each color print unique and individual. Azarian has illustrated several picture books, including *Snowflake Bentley*, for which she was awarded the 1999 Caldecott Award. Azarian currently makes her home in Vermont.

Artist

Carpenter, Nancy

Now living in Brooklyn, New York with her husband and daughter (Maeve), Nancy Carpenter is the illustrator of several books, including *Washing the Willow Tree Loon* by Jacqueline Briggs Martin. After graduating from college, Carpenter became a "graphic reporter" creating maps and charts. She became acquainted with some children's publishing art directors and soon was encouraged to submit some illustrations. She did, and soon was offered a book contract. Now she has paints, pens, brushes, and reference books throughout her house. Carpenter's illustrations, often described as bright and full of spirit, are more realistic and more sophisticated than in picture books intended for the very young reader.

Artist

Gaber, Susan

Susan Gaber grew up in Brooklyn, New York and after attending Long Island College she became a freelance illustrator. In 1991, she was asked by two different publishers to illustrate a book written by Jacqueline Briggs Martin. In the spring of 1992 those two books, *Good Times on Grandfather Mountain* and *The Finest Horse in Town*, were published. In 2003, *The Finest Horse in Town* was republished by Purple House Press. Her illustrations are often described as being in a "folk style" and rendered in a jewel tone palette, although sometimes muted. She works in watercolor and colored pencil on Strathmore Bristol paper. She continues to live and work in New York state.

Artist
Gillman, Alec

Alec Gillman (Alexander Gillman), a former resident of Ipswich, New York, now resides in the Berkshire Hills of western Massachusetts and is an environmental educator with the Massachusetts Department of Conservation and Recreation. In 2005, Gillman was at the Mount Greylock State Reservation where he regularly speaks to school groups about environmental topics. Gillman grew up in Boxford, Massachusetts and studied at the Pratt Institute, where he was trained in communication and design. He illustrated several books, including, in 1997, Jacqueline Briggs Martin's *Green Truck Garden Giveaway: A Neighborhood Story and Almanac.* His illustrations are created with pen and ink with watercolors and pencil. The small-town setting was actually, according to Gillman, a little bit of Brooklyn and Boston, and of his hometown of Boxford. The people were, in some cases, drawn with reference to a few of his relatives and friends.

Artist
Johnson, David A.

David A. Johnson is a talented illustrator who has been drawing in line since he was a high-school student in New Canaan, Connecticut. He began his freelance illustrative work at the age of nineteen. His detailed pen-and-ink portraits still appear regularly In the *New York Times Book Review, Time, Harvard Business Review, The Atlantic Monthly,* and other prestigious publications. In addition to his editorial illustrations, he has illustrated several children's books, including Jacqueline Briggs Martin's *On Sand Island* in 2004. His own love of boating and being in the water brought him to this story and the decision to illustrate it—his first book for Houghton Mifflin. His illustrations are created with pen and ink with watercolor. After spending his early years in Detroit where he was born, Johnson moved with his family to New Canaan, Connecticut, where he currently lives and works.

Artist
Krommes, Beth

Beth Krommes creates illustrations with scratchboard and watercolors. She began using the scratchboard technique after working with wood engraving for many years. The scratchboard technique is much faster but has a similar look. Her path to children's books began in the world of fine art. Then she went into commercial art and finally, now, to illustrating children's books. She admires the illustrative work of James Marshall, Barbara Cooney, and others, as well as enjoying folk art and the art of the Eskimo and Inuit. It is the art of those cultures that inspired the art she used for the illustrations of *The Lamp, the Ice, and the Boat Called Fish*. In 2001, the Society of Children's Book Writers and Illustrators awarded her the Golden Kite Award for the illustrations for that book. In creating the illustrations, Krommes first carves images into a linoleum block and then dips the carving into black ink and photocopies those pieces. Color is added to the photocopies with watercolor. Much of her art is based on the research she does to learn about appropriate cultures, some of her inspiration also comes from her daughters, Olivia and Marguerite, who sometimes make their appearance in the illustrations she creates. Beth Krommes lives and works in Peterborough, New Hampshire.

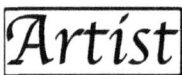

Mathers, Petra

Petra Mathers was born shortly after World War II in Todtmoos, Germany—a town nestled in the Black Forest. In Germany she was an apprentice in the book business. At the age of twenty-three she came to the United States and settled in Portland, Oregon, where she worked in a friend's bookstore. It was during her bookstore days that she came to appreciate the picture book format and decided she would try creating a book of her own. Her first illustrations were published in 1983, and as an illustrator she has created illustrations for books she has written as well as books written by other writers, such as Jacqueline Briggs Martin's *Grandmother Bryant's Pocket*. Her illustrations have garnered the *New York Times* prize for Best Illustrated Children's Book, four times, and the Ezra Jack Keats Medal. Her illustrations for *Grandmother Bryant's Pocket* combine her naïve and flat styles and a style reminiscent of American folklore. Mathers and her husband currently live in Astoria, Oregon.

Artist

Ormai, Stella

Stella Ormai used pen and ink with watercolor to illustrate the three Bizzy Bones books by Jacqueline Briggs Martin. Her creative map end papers complemented her realistic and detailed depictions of Bizzy Bones and his patient Uncle Ezra and their community of friends. Ormai illustrated a dozen or so books in the late 1980s and early 1990s. She lives in Providence, Rhode Island.

Redenbaugh, Vicki Jo

Vicki Jo Redenbaugh is a children's book illustrator and a blueberry farmer. She and her husband, David Martinsen, operate Red Oaks Farm on the Wisconsin Bayfield Peninsula that juts out into Lake Superior near the Apostle Islands (coincidentally the site of Jacqueline Briggs Martin's *On Sand Island*). The blueberries are raised on a 1-acre plot set among 90 acres of trees. David builds custom furniture and cabinets from lumber on their land. Together they are raising their two children (Arnie and Esme) and tending the blueberry patches, and Vicki continues to illustrate children's books, mostly for Carolrhoda books in Minneapolis. Her illustrations for *Button, Bucket, Sky* are realistically rendered with a soft pastel palette. Redenbaugh's family has grown oak trees from acorns—something that is part of Jacqueline Briggs Martin's *Button, Bucket, Sky*.

Root, Barry

Barry Root has illustrated many books, including Jacqueline Briggs Martin's and her daughter Sarah's *Banjo Granny's Song*. Root's illustrations are characteristically energetic and light. He and his wife, Kimberly Bulcken Root, also an illustrator, live in Quarryfield, Lancaster County, Pennsylvania with their three children and several dogs.

Sneed, Brad

Bradley D. Sneed is a proud native of Kansas, a state where he still lives today. He grew up in the country in a big white house with trees to climb and horses to ride. From a very young age he often could be found drawing. He entered his drawings in the county fair and during his high-school years he even sold some of his paintings. After graduating from high school, he entered Kansas University to study illustrations, and at the end of his senior year, he headed to New York to show his portfolio to editors. He came home with a contract to illustrate his first book. Now he has illustrated more than twenty books and continues to live in Kansas. He and his family (a wife and daughter, along with a dog, two rats, and a gecko) live near Kansas City, where he continues to draw and paint.

Artist
Sweet, Melissa

For more than twenty years Melissa Sweet has been illustrating children's books. Her art work is always a little different for each book she helps to create. Her art is often described as being "whimsical watercolors," but she regularly incorporates collage and technical details—whatever is appropriate to the specific title. She has created the illustrations for Jacqueline's *Chicken Joy on Redbean Road*.

Sweet was raised in Wyckoff, New Jersey and studied at Endicott junior College in Massachusetts before entering a commercial art program at the Kansas City Art Institute. Her first illustrative commissions were for posters, greeting cards, and one-of-a-kind handmade books. Her entry into the world of children's books began, in 1985, when she assembled an art portfolio and went to New York City to meet with art editors. It was during that first trip that she was asked to create illustrations for an early reading series. Since that time, she has illustrated more than sixty children's books, often with cartoon-like very light watercolors. She has begun to write some of her own stories. She lives with her husband and stepdaughter near a working harbor in Rockport, Maine. Her studio is nearby.

Artist
Wingerter, Linda S.

Growing up in a creative family, Linda S. Wingerter, was encouraged from a very young age to express herself as an artist. She admired the work of Trina Schart Hyman and other picture book artists and decided at age four that she wanted to become a children's book artist. She studied at the Rhode Island School of Design and studied in Europe during her junior year. As a freelance artist her work has appeared in financial publications, in novels, on posters, in textbooks, and in a host of other venues. Since 1994, she has also exhibited her work at several galleries. Wingerter's acrylic illustrations for Jacqueline Briggs Martin's *The Water Gift and the Pig of the Pig* have been described as being "swathed in soothing, subdued blues, greens," "lushly textured," having a "nostalgic feel . . . in an antique palette," and "striking a balance between folk art and nods to some of the American masters."

Wingerter spent her growing up years on a horse farm in Maine and Vermont. She now lives in West Haven, Connecticut in a ninety-year-old house that she is renovating.

An Author's Letter to YOU!

Dear Readers

When I visit schools, people sometimes say to me, "You're a writer. I hate to write." I want to stop right there—in the hallway, in the library, or in the lunchroom, wherever we are—sit down with them, and have a conversation about writing. I think we say we hate to write when we have not figured out what we really want to write. This book is my part of the conversation I would like to have. I have written it so that students can use it by themselves or teachers can share it with students as a group project. I hope there will be many ways to have a part in this conversation.

Some readers may come to this book because they want to think about writing in a new way. Some may come because they have read some of my books and want to know more about them. Learning what I think of writing will help anyone know my books better. Some may come to this book to know me better. Because writing is so important in my life, you will find much of me in this book.

I want to talk in this book about how writing can be fun and how we can learn to write about what's important to us. Once writing becomes fun, we find more and better ways to write.

But I also have to say right here at the beginning that I think writing is like bicycle riding. I could never learn to ride a bicycle just by reading what others said about how to ride a bicycle. They might write that bicycle riding is lots of fun and tell me where I could go on my bike. They might tell me how a bicycle is constructed or who have been great bike riders. They might write about balance and how it's easier to balance if you are pedaling faster. And even if I read every word, I would not be able to ride a bicycle.

I had to get on my bicycle, try it, fall down, get up, and get on again. Eventually I learned to ride. You and I cannot get to our best writing only by reading what others say about writing. We can get better by reading. I want to share with you some of my writing experiences. But to get to our best writing we have to sit down and write. So, your part in the conversation will be to do some writing. Let's get started.

Sincerely,

Jacqueline Briggs Martin

Why Write?

Writing is not just an exercise that someone tells me to do. Writing helps me notice what's around me, helps me figure out my place in the world. It helps me think about what I like and what I don't like.

Imagine waking up in the morning. At first your head is groggy, you can hardly hear what people are saying to you, you are not really aware of what is in your room. As you become more awake, you notice more and hear better. Your brain starts to respond to what you notice and what you hear. You realize that your Dad is saying, "Breakfast is ready." Then you realize you smell toast, and you hear your sister asking for strawberry jam. Writing helps me to "wake up" to what is going on around me.

When I keep a notebook, I notice more. I might notice the man and woman at the park on the corner who always feed the pigeons on Thursdays. I might notice that they actually have names for the pigeons. Perhaps they have named them for nursery rhyme characters—Jack Horner, Little Bo Peep, Humpty Dumpty. But there's one named Blanche. I would wonder why. And I might begin to imagine why they would feed the pigeons; give them names; name one Blanche. I try to have a journal handy so I can always write down my questions. Perhaps the pigeons with their nursery rhyme names will show up in a story some day. New ideas often bring even more new ideas.

Writing is also a way that I have a conversation with myself. This conversation can work in many ways.

- Sometimes the conversation that we have by writing helps us decide how to spend time. When our son Justin was young, he wrote series of notes to himself. One was "when you are bored." Another was "when you are angry."

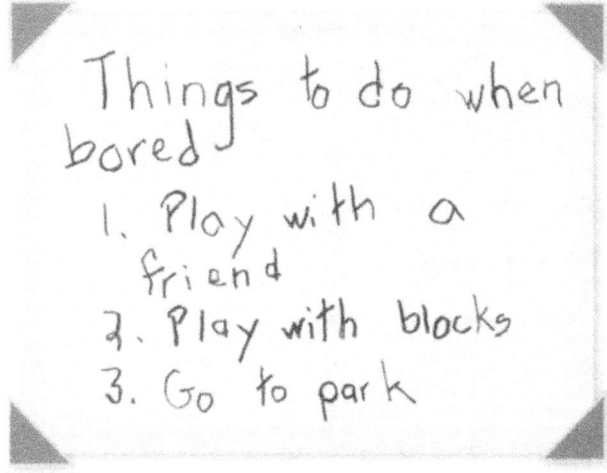

- Sometimes writing can help solve problems. When our daughter Sarah was in first grade, she walked to school. On her route was a barking dog that always worried her. She was able to find a "dog-free" route and avoid the dog. But if she had not done that she might have written a note to herself—"ways to solve the barking-dog problem." And she might have continued:
  1. Walk with Mom or Dad.
  2. Walk with a friend.
- Writing can be a way of having fun, just being silly with words. Here are some ways I have fun with words:
  - I once had a job writing spelling books and I used to spend time writing lists of rhyming words. Here's part of one of my lists:

  - When I was in elementary school, a teacher gave us the assignment to write down all the words we could think of that sounded the same but are not spelled the same. I still keep that list and add to it—in my head. Here's part of it:

- Sometimes it's fun to make up new words for new ideas or new objects. In my first book, *Bizzy Bones and Uncle Ezra*, Bizzy makes a "whichdoodle" with scraps of wood. A whichdoodle is a made-up word, which means something you make by doodling around. It can be made whichever way you want to make it. You might want to make up a word for the mixture you make when you stir peanut butter and jam together or the scary noise of a squeaky door.

Bizzy Bones creates a "whichdoodle" from scraps of wood.

Filling the Room We Call Our Imagination

Writing is a way to put more furniture in that room I call my imagination.
- I can imagine the breakfast conversation between the couple who always feed the pigeons and write it in my notebook.
- I can imagine where my cat went in those three days when she wasn't at home.
- I can imagine where my cat goes at night.

A richer imagination helps me understand what life might be like for the new neighbor on the block, or the person who drives the school bus past my house.

A richer imagination means I have more ideas when I need them, when I want to solve problems or help a friend, when I want to write a story.

The best part of writing for me is that I get to tell stories, stories of real people or stories about people who come from my imagination. Since I was a child with an imaginary playmate, I have loved stories and the sounds of words. I think I will always love coming up with new characters and wondering how they would solve problems.

> **Books: The Best Writing Teachers**
>
> Writers are always hoping to get better. We never think we know all there is to know about writing. One way we learn about how to be better writers is to read good books. When I have a writing problem, I read the picture books I love so I can learn how others have solved similar problems. I don't copy their books, but sometimes the stories of others help me think in a new way. At the end of each section of this book, you'll find a list of books that may be helpful to you.

Writing: Work or Play? When to Write? What to Write?

Writing as Play, Writing for Fun

My friends who don't like to write think all writing is work. But by the time they have finished this book they will understand that we can also write for fun. Writing for fun is the writing we do for ourselves. I've already mentioned the fun of noticing words. It might also be fun to write a list of tricks your dog can do. For me, it might be fun to write a list of things I like to do at the park with my grandson Owen.

> List of things Owen and I do at the park:
> 1. Run.
> 2. Stand at the water plaza and get wet.
> 3. Sit on the grass and eat sandwiches.
> 4. Count butterflies.
> 5. Write on the sidewalk with chalk.
> 6. Go down the curvy slide eight times.

Fun writing might also be a list of things that make me jump-up-and-down happy, angry, or sad. Fun writing might be writing about a best friend or wondering who's going to move into the empty house next door. Or it might be going to the same tree on the corner every day at four o'clock and writing down who walks by. Fun writing might be keeping a list of jokes.

Writing the stories I write is fun writing for me. I write about what interests me. I write about subjects I want to think about for the whole time (often years) it takes me to write a book.

The writing we do for ourselves is just that—writing for ourselves. The only rule is that we *want* to write it. In the beginning of writing a story I don't have to use complete sentences. I don't have to spell correctly. I only have to spell close enough that I can read what I have written a few days later. I can say whatever I want to say.

When I decide I want to share my writing with others, I have to spell the words correctly and work to choose the best words to say what I want to say.

Writing as Work

"Writing for work" might be writing that I do for regular pay. People who write as their job are newspaper reporters, writers of "how-to" manuals, cookbook writers, catalogue writers, television commercial writers, and many others.

Sometimes these writers may be writing about a topic that is not at the top of their "this really interests me" list, but the topic is interesting to others, so someone is paying them to do the writing. Perhaps they are writing a "how to build a doghouse" manual or writing reports of research about why people want to do certain jobs.

Though I do not dream about heavy construction equipment, I have written many articles about bulldozers, excavators, and front-end loaders. And I realized in doing that writing that I enjoyed finding the right words to say something about how these machines work.

For some, "writing for work" might be writing that is assigned at school. It might be a report on a person or a period of history that at first doesn't seem very interesting. It might be an assignment to make up a story. There are ways to make writing for work much more like writing for fun. We'll be looking at some of those ways later on in this book.

When to Write

The best time to write is different for each person. When I was a child the only writing I did was school writing, except for one essay on why farmers should keep registered Holstein cows. I usually did not write at home. I never thought about keeping my own writing notebook.

Writing is an everyday activity.
Photo credit:
Sharron L. McElmeel.

Now, I keep many writing notebooks and my favorite time of the day to work on stories is early in the morning. I like to get up before the sun comes up, make one cup of coffee, say "Hello, how are you," to my husband, and sit down with my writing.

But I have also written in my notebooks in the afternoon on airplanes, under the trees at noontime on Sand Island, at night in hotel rooms, on buses, and in the middle of busy convention halls.

I have author friends who don't start their writing until after they've eaten dinner and washed the dishes. They start writing late at night when all the others in their houses are in bed.

What to Write: Where do I Find Ideas for Writing?

Sometimes I get a wonderful idea while I am busy brushing my teeth or mowing the yard. When I take out my notebook and sit down to write, it's gone. My wonderful idea has just evaporated from my brain. I stare at my notebook and get no ideas. This happens to all writers. There are times when our "idea cupboard" is as bare as Old Mother Hubbard's cupboard. For those times it's nice to have a list of suggestions. I keep a file of stories that I'd like to know more about. When my idea cupboard is bare, I go to that file. When I find a story or question in that file that makes me want to know more, my idea cupboard begins to fill. As I share the stories of my stories in this book you will notice that I have found ideas in my family, in magazines, in books, from the things I love, and from the things I worry about.

Writing Longer Pieces

Writing about a Favorite Place

We all can think of favorite places, places where we go when we want to be alone, or places that make us feel better when we're feeling bad, or places where we remember good times.

When I was growing up I had a favorite place on a hill, along a dirt lane from our farm buildings, in a grove of pine trees. I liked to walk the lane and sit under the trees.

A dirt lane leads away from Jacqueline's farm home—and to a favorite place.

My list of what I loved about this place would have looked like this:

Things I like about my favorite place, the pine grove:
1. The sound of the breeze through the trees.
2. I can see the sky between the trees.
3. The pine needles make a soft place to sit.
4. I feel as if I am in a very big room with space to stretch out.
5. I can hear birds.
6. I can hear what I am thinking.
7. This place lets me wonder what my father and my grandfather and my grandfather's grandfather did when they were children on this farm.

Cabin on Sand Island.

I have always loved places with lots of trees, and still do. One of my current favorite places is Sand Island in the Apostle Islands.

> The Apostle Islands are a group of Islands in Lake Superior, off the northern edge of Wisconsin. They now make up the Apostle Islands National Lakeshore.

I was happy to go and live in a cabin on Sand Island for twelve days. And because I love the place so much I wanted to write a story about it.

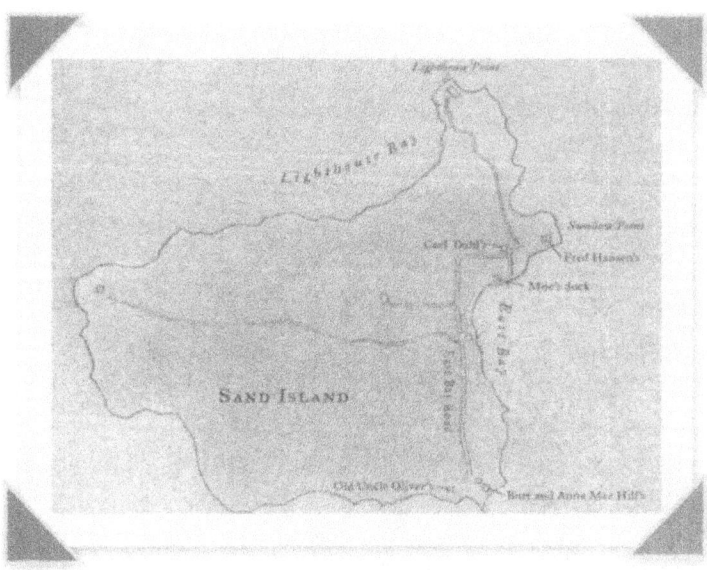

A map of Sand Island shows the location of some of the important places.

Things I like about Sand Island:
1. Watching the waves on Lake Superior.
2. Watching birds land on the water.
3. Listening to the breezes in the trees around our cabin.
4. Picking blueberries out by the lighthouse.
5. Watching the rabbits outside our cabin.
6. Bailing water out of the lake and boiling it (to kill germs) for our coffee.
7. Being inside the cabin during a howling windstorm.
8. The journal out at the lighthouse that tells the story of the lighthouse keeper and his wife.

Things I'm not so sure about
1. Bathing in a bucket.
2. Mosquitos, mosquitos, mosquitos.

A tree lined cove on the Sand Island.
Photo Credit: Jacqueline Briggs Martin

Sand Island lighthouse.

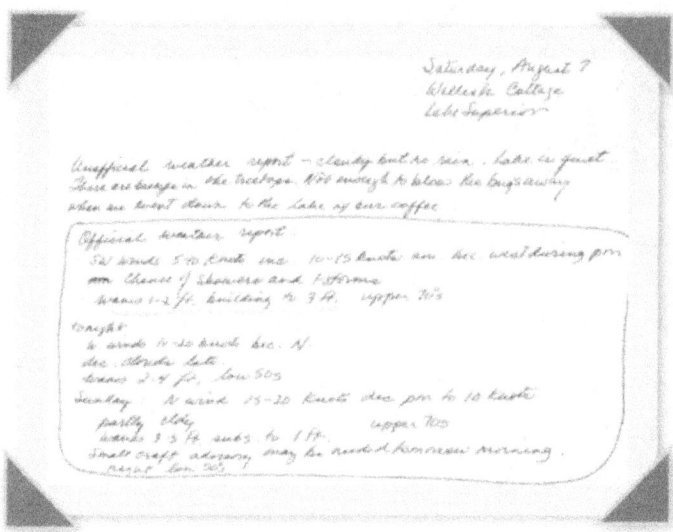

Portion of journal written while on the island.

While I was on Sand Island I wanted to learn as much about the island as I could. I wanted to know the history of the island—the stories of the people who had lived there in past times. I wanted to walk the island, taste the blueberries that grew by the lighthouse, watch the sun come up on the eastern side of the island, walk the island by moonlight.

In my Sand Island journal I wrote down everything that happened—the weather reports that came over our two-way radio each day, the little spider that crawled into the outhouse bathroom, the walks I took, even my wonderings about the other people who had lived in the cabin before us.

While I was on the island I talked to people who had lived there. I asked them questions, and wrote down the answers.

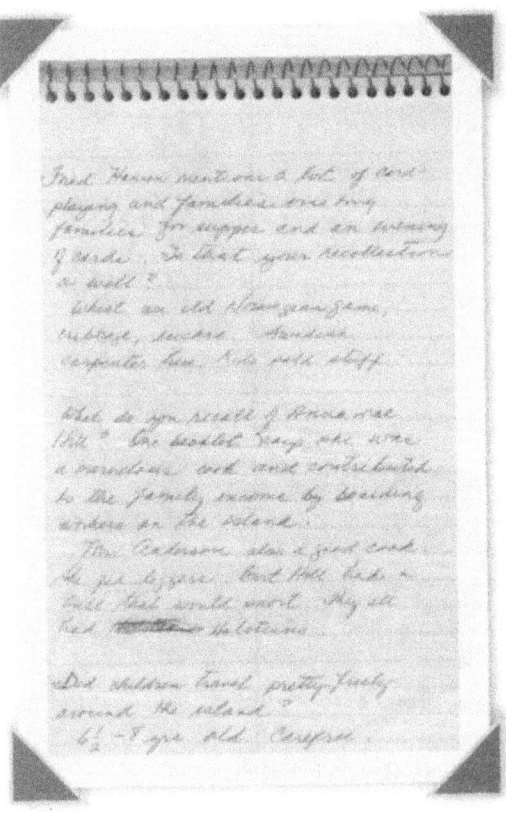

I listened as they told me stories that were important to them. One story that everyone remembered was the story of Harold Dahl, who had drowned in Lake Superior in April 1928. All the fishermen had gone out on that first day of fishing in 1928. A storm came up. Harold Dahl had trouble starting his engine but waved at the others to signal they should head for home. The other fishermen made it back to Sand Island. Harold Dahl was never seen again. Many people told me that story, and I realized that the story of Harold Dahl was as much a part of Sand Island as the trees and the rocks.

The people I talked with also told me the story of farmer Noring's fierce bull, which would break through the fence and run around the island.

Others had interviewed men and women who had lived on Sand Island. I read those interviews and learned about people I could not talk with. I heard of Annamae Hill's wonderful cooking, including the coconut cream cake.

When I wrote the book *On Sand Island* I included many of the details I had learned about Sand Island. I wrote about one boy's love of boats, about Annamae Hill's wonderful coconut cream cake, about Burt Hill's ability to make do with what he had, about Fred Hanson. Because fishing was so important on Sand Island I wanted to include details of fishing—nets, net reels. I could not find a place in the story to put the bull that chased children around the island.

Booklist

A Sampling: Books about Place

Addy, Sharon Hart. *Right Here on This Spot.* Illustrated by John Clapp. Houghton Mifflin, 1999.

Atwell, Debby. *Barn.* Houghton Mifflin, 2001.

Cooney, Barbara. *Island Boy.* Puffin Reprint, 1991.

Geisert, Bonnie. *River Town* (1999); *Desert Town* (2001); *Prairie Town* (1998); and *Mountain Town* (2000). Illustrated by Arthur Geisert. Houghton Mifflin.

Hall, Donald. *Old Home Day.* Illustrated by Emily Arnold McCully. Browndeer, 1994.

Kurtz, Jane. *Faraway Home.* Illustrated by E. B. Lewis. Gulliver/Harcourt, 2000.

Lyon, George Ella. *Dreamplace.* Illustrated by Peter Catalanotto. Orchard Books, 1993.

Martin, Charles. *Island Winter.* William Morrow, 1994.

Martin, Jacqueline Briggs. *On Sand Island.* Illustrated by David A. Johnson. Houghton Mifflin, 2003.

McLerran, Alice. *Roxaboxen.* Illustrated by Barbara Cooney. Lothrop, Lee & Shepard, 1990.

Sorensen, Henri. *New Hope.* Lothrop, Lee & Shepard, 1995.

Vizurraga, Susan. *Miss Opal's Auction.* Illustrated by Mark Graham. Henry Holt, 2000.

Yolen, Jane. *Letting Swift River Go.* Illustrated by Barbara Cooney. Little, Brown, 1992.

Writing about a Person

For many of us there is a person, or people, whom we are glad to see. They make us smile when we think of them. Maybe they remember the things that are important to us—that we like ice cubes in our milk, catsup on eggs, and we love reading.

Maybe they are good listeners. Maybe they love to do the same things we love to do. Maybe they are *really* good at doing what we love to do and we would like to be just like them.

Maybe they live close to us and we see them every day. Maybe they live far away and we've never seen them, but we think about them, they are part of what a writer named C. S. Lewis called "the furniture of our minds."

There are people, too, who are interesting to us. Perhaps they have hobbies we've never heard of. Perhaps they have jobs we'd like to know more about. Perhaps they had to solve a problem or overcome an obstacle like one we are faced with.

There are also people we call our heroes. They do the things we admire, the things we would like to do.

Writing about My "Hero"

Wilson Bentley is one of my heroes. He was born in 1865 on a small farm in Vermont and he grew up to be a farmer, too. But he did not love farming. He loved taking pictures of single snowflakes. He had to teach himself the technique because no one in his little town knew how to use a camera with a microscope attached. Once he learned, he took more than 5000 pictures of individual snow crystals.

One of Bentley's snow crystal photographs.

I admire Wilson Bentley because he did what he wanted to do—take pictures of snow crystals—even though his neighbors and friends may have thought he was odd. He continued to take his pictures because he could see beauty in snow crystals and wanted to share that beauty with others. He did not stop because he wasn't getting rich. He did not stop because he wasn't famous. He did what he loved just because *he* thought it was important.

I decided a few years ago that I wanted to write a book for children about Wilson Bentley (known in Vermont as "Snowflake" Bentley).

Of course I wanted to interview Mr. Bentley, but I couldn't. He had died in 1931. I had a list of questions, but I could not ask them. I read to find the answers to my questions. I read articles that Wilson Bentley had published in magazines and newspapers. I read what others wrote about him. I read about farming in New England during the time Wilson Bentley was growing up. I learned that Wilson Bentley, from his earliest memories, had loved snow more than anything else in the world ("except his mother," he said). I learned that he lived in a house he shared with his brother Charlie and Charlie's family, and that he also loved music. He never married.

I wanted my research to be more than reading. I wanted to see the shed where he worked. I wanted to stand in his dooryard and look at Bolton Mountain just as he would have. So I went to Maine and my mother and I drove to Vermont. I talked with Ray Miglionico, archivist at the Jericho Historical Society. He showed me Wilson Bentley's camera, some of his photographs, and a quilt that Willie's mother had made for him. Mr Miglionico also took me to the house where Wilson Bentley lived his life. The family who now lives there invited us in to look at the house. I stood in the shed and imagined Willie making his photos. I went into the kitchen and imagined him sitting by a warm stove on a cold winter's night.

Illustrator Mary Azarian's picture of the Bentley farm.

By the time I came back to my home in Iowa I was ready to begin to write. Doing the research for a book is in some ways easier than doing the writing. To do the research I think of what I know about a subject and what I would like to know. I write down what I would like to know. Often answering those questions leads to more questions. I add those to my list and continue to try to find answers.

Doing the writing is not quite so "make-a-list-and-do-the-list" as doing research. Often we have to write something wrong before we know how to write it right. We have to choose wrong words before the best words come into our heads. In writing the story of Wilson Bentley I wrote several versions before I wrote the text that you can read in the book. In the first version I wrote about just one snowy day in Wilson Bentley's life. In the book, the story covers his life from childhood until he dies—and after.

Booklist

A Sampling: Books about People

Many family stories feature the "people" in our families, so those books (listed later) would work in this section as well. These stories/poems about people tend to be longer works that authors have researched and written because they wanted to know more about a historical person. Most of these are biographical or based on an actual person's life. However, there are "stories" that authors have made up as well.

Anderson, M. T. *Handel, Who Knew What He Liked.* Candlewick, 2002.

Andrews-Goebel, Nancy. *The Pot That Juan Built.* Illustrated by David Diaz. Lee and Low, 2002.

Best, Cari. *Three Cheers for Catherine the Great!* Illustrated by Giselle Potter. Melanie Kroupa/DK Ink, 1999.

Blumberg, Rhoda. *York's Adventures with Lewis and Clark: An African-American's Part in the Great Expedition.* HarperCollins, 2005.

Burleigh, Robert. *Lookin' for Bird in the Big City.* Illustrated by Marek Los. Silver Whistle/Harcourt, 2001.

Brumbeau, Jeff. *The Quilt Maker's Journey.* Illustrated by Gail de Marcken. Orchard Books, Spring, 2005.

Burleigh, Robert. *Seurat and La Grande Jatte: Connecting the Dots.* Abrams Books for Young Readers, 2004.

Christensen, Bonnie. *Woody Guthrie: Poet of the People.* Knopf, 2002.

Davidson, Margaret. *The Story of Jackie Robinson: Bravest Man in Baseball.* Illustrated by Floyd Cooper. Gareth Stevens, 1996.

Fradin, Dennis Brindell, and Judith Bloom Fradin. *Ida B. Wells: Mother of the Civil Rights Movement.* Clarion, 2000.

Giblin, James Cross. *Good Brother, Bad Brother: The Story of Edwin Booth and John Wilkes Booth.* Clarion, 2005.

Hopkinson, Deborah. *A Band of Angels: A Story Inspired by the Jubilee Singers.* Illustrated by Raul Colon. Atheneum Books for Young Readers, 1999.

Hopkinson, Deborah. *Fannie in the Kitchen: The Whole Story from Soup to Nuts of How Fannie Farmer Invented Recipes with Precise Measurements.* Illustrated by Nancy Carpenter. Simon & Schuster/Anne Schwartz, 2001.

Hopkinson, Deborah. *Girl Wonder: A Baseball Story in Nine Innings.* Illustrated by Terry Widener. Simon & Schuster/Atheneum, 2003.

Hughes, Susan. *Earth to Audrey.* Illustrated by Stephanie Poulin. Kids Can Press, 2005.

Kulling, Monica. *Great Houdini.* Illustrated by Anne Reas. Random House, 1999.

Lasky, Kathryn. *The Librarian Who Measured the Earth.* Illustrated by Kevin Hawkes. Little, Brown, 1994.

Meyer, Kerstin. *Pirate Girl.* Chicken House/Scholastic, 2005.

Nelson, Marilyn. *Carver: A Life in Poems.* Front Street Books, 2001.

Pinkney, Andrea Davis. *Bill Pickett: Rodeo-Ridin' Cowboy.* Illustrated by Brian Pinkney. Harcourt/Gulliver, 1996.

Pinkney, Andrea Davis. *Dear Benjamin Banneker.* Illustrated by Brian Pinkney. Harcourt/Gulliver, 1994.

Rumford, James. *Seeker of Knowledge: The Man Who Deciphered Egyptian Hieroglyphs.* Houghton Mifflin, 2000.

Ryan, Pam Muñoz. *When Marian Sang: The True Recital of Marian Anderson.* Illustrated by Brian Selznick. Scholastic, 2002.

Smith, Cynthia Leitech. *Jingle Dancer.* Illustrated by Cornelius Van Wright and Ying-Hwa Hu. Morrow, 2000.

Winter, Jeanette. *The Librarian of Basra: A True Story from Iraq.* Harcourt, 2004.

Writing a Family Story

Every family has stories. And one of the fun things about writing a family story is that we already know the people who can tell us more details of the family story.

Writing My Family Story

When I was young my mother taught me to sew. While we were working she told me the story of her aunt Zilpha who had taught her to sew (her own mother had died when my mother was a baby).

Zilpha and her sister Stella were wonderful seamstresses and owned a dry-goods store in a small town in Maine in the 1890s. They sold gloves and socks, cloth and corsets, needles and pins and all kinds of shoes, and they sewed dresses for their customers. When they retired from storekeeping, they moved to California because the climate was better for Stella. After Stella died, Zilpha moved back to Maine. That was when she taught my mother to sew. She showed my mother how to make small, even stitches and told her not to be satisfied with sloppy work. My mother taught me to make small, even stitches and told me not to be satisfied with sloppy work.

When I was grown I wanted to know more about the sisters' store in Norway, Maine. One summer day when my daughter, Sarah, was about ten years old, Sarah, my mother, and I went to Norway. We found the place where the store had been. Then we went to the library and we found some newspapers from the 1890s. In those newspapers we saw advertisements from the sisters' store.

We felt as if we were getting close to the store but we wanted to know more. We wanted some details from someone who actually remembered the store.

The librarian told us to go down the street and talk to the jeweler, who was ninety-two years old. She said he might remember the store. We did talk to him and he did remember. He said the sisters had the finest horse in town. He told us the sisters liked to take the horse out for a drive on Wednesday afternoon and Sunday afternoon.

Zilpha was one of my aunts. Our family photo album does not include a photograph of Stella.

After our Maine vacation, back in Iowa, I decided I wanted to write about these sisters. I thought about what I knew.

The store's sign reads "S. B. & Z. S. Prince" Prince was my aunt's family name.

I knew I wanted to write about the two sisters.

The two sisters are the characters. Would there be other characters? I didn't know yet. In a small town others would have known about the horse. So I thought there should be other characters.

I knew the small town in Maine where the sisters lived would be the setting.

The sisters' dry goods store would also be part of the setting. They sold gloves and socks, cloth and corsets, needles and pins, and all kinds of shoes.

I knew why this story was important to me.

These two sisters were kind to my mother, so they were important to me. I wanted to spend time thinking about them and telling their story.

I knew some details of sight, sound, taste, and smell that would be part of this story.

Sight—the horse. What did he look like? The buggy.

The store.

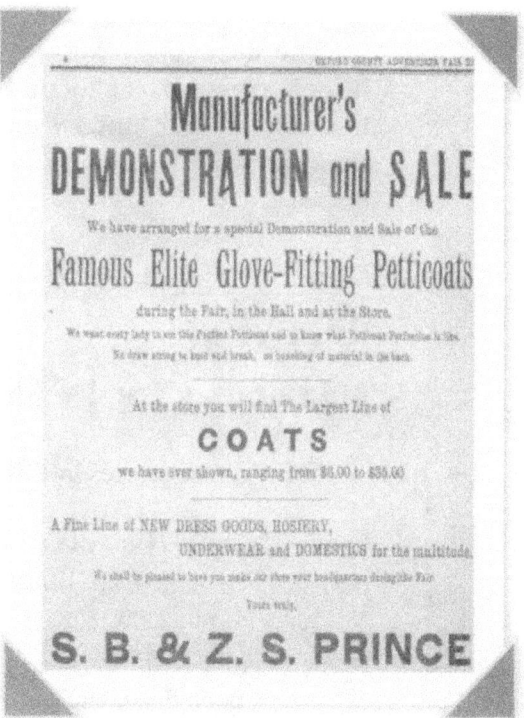

This is an advertisement, for my aunt's store, which we found in one of the newspapers that we located in the library.

From the newspaper advertisement I knew what they sold. I could include that in the story.

From my mother I know the sisters worked hard. I could include that in the story.

I didn't know any details about what might have happened during the drives on Wednesday and Sunday.

I didn't know any details about what others thought about the horse. I would have to make those up.

What did I know that would help me make up the details I needed? What could I remember?

I remembered my grandfather talking about cattle traders. And that made me think there must have been horse traders, too.

I remembered when some of the cattle on our farm ate lead paint and died. That made me think the "finest horse" could eat something that would make him sick.

What I have in my head, in my memory are the things I use in my writing. All of the things I know of, or remember, or worry about, or laugh about are like a big storeroom where I can go and find details for my writing.

The story of these sisters became my book *The Finest Horse in Town*. It took almost a year to answer these questions, to add the details that I needed to add. But I wanted to tell this story—partly because these sisters were important to my family and because I have always loved horses.

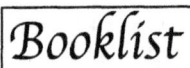

A Sampling: Family Stories in Books

Many of the stories in this list are based on actual family experiences.

Cooney, Barbara. *Hattie and the Wild Waves.* Viking, 1990.

de Paola, Tomie. *Nana Upstairs and Nana Downstairs.* Putnam 1987. Putnam, 1998. Puffin, 2000 (paper).

Felipe Herrera, Juan. *Grandma and Me at the Flea/Los Meros Meros Remateros.* Children's Book Press, 2002.

Helmer, Marilyn. *One Special Tree.* Illustrated by Dianne Eastman. Kids Can Press, 2005.

Houston, Gloria. *My Great Aunt Arizona.* HarperCollins, 1992.

Houston, Gloria. *The Year of the Perfect Christmas Tree.* New York: Dial, 1988.

Howard, Elizabeth Fitzgerald. *Papa Tells Chita a Story.* Simon & Schuster, 1995.

Hurst, Carol Otis. *Rocks in His Head.* Illustrated by James Stevenson. Greenwillow, 2001.

Lasky, Kathryn. *Marven of the Great Northwoods.* Harcourt, Brace & Co., 1997.

Look, Lenore. *Love As Strong As Ginger.* Atheneum, 1999.

Martin, Jacqueline Briggs. *The Finest Horse in Town.* HarperCollins, 1992; Purple House Press, 2003.

Mathers, Petra. *Kisses from Rosa.* Knopf, 1995.

Pak, Soyung. *A Place to Grow.* Levine/Scholastic, 2002.

Pinkney, Andrea Davis. *Mim's Christmas Jam.* Illustrated by Brian Pinkney. Harcourt/Gulliver, 2001.

Pinkney, Gloria Jean. *Back Home.* Dial, 1992.

Pittman, Helena Clare. *Uncle Phil's Diner.* Carolrhoda, 1998.

Polacco, Patricia. *Keeping Quilt.* Simon & Schuster, 1988. (Note: Since this very early family story, Polacco has written and illustrated dozens of additional titles. Many of the titles she has created are based on family stories and may be used in conjunction with any focus on writing family stories.)

Rylant, Cynthia. *Christmas in the Country.* Blue Sky, Scholastic, 2002.

Rylant, Cynthia. *The Relatives Came.* Bradbury Press, 1985.

Rylant, Cynthia. *When I Was Young in the Mountains.* Dutton, 1982.

Say, Allen. *Grandfather's Journey.* Houghton Mifflin, 1993.

Say, Allen. *Tea with Milk.* Houghton Mifflin, 1999.

Warhola, James. *Uncle Andy's.* Putnam, 2003.

Woodson, Jacqueline. *Coming on Home Soon.* Illustrated by E. B. Lewis. Putnam, 2004.

Yolen, Jane. *Owl Moon.* Illustrated by John Schoenerr. Philomel, 1987.

Nonfiction

Research for *The Lamp, the Ice, and the Boat Called* Fish

A few years ago, I read of two young girls and a little black cat that were part of the Canadian Arctic Expedition of 1913. During this expedition a boat sailed north to the Arctic Sea. The expedition leader, Vilhjalmur Stefansson, hoped to discover new land and become famous. When the boat reached Barrow, Alaska—340 miles north of the Arctic Circle, Stefansson hired Iñupiaq men to join the party as hunters. He also needed a woman to sew warm boots and clothes for the scientists and crew. A man named Kurulluk and his wife, Qiruk, agreed to join the party. They had two children, Pagnasuk (eight years old) and Makpii (two years old). The boat eventually became trapped in winter ice. Stefansson left the group. They lived for a while on a large piece of ice, then traveled to Wrangel Island. Without Kurulluk's hunting and Qiruk's careful sewing, many explorers and scientists on the expedition would not have survived. When I read of this family I knew right away I wanted to learn more. I knew I wanted to write a story for children about this family and the journey of the *Karluk*.

I thought of some questions I would need to answer before I could write about this story. Here are a few from my list:

1. What did the people do after their boat was trapped in the ice?
2. What did they eat while on the boat? While they lived on the ice? After they went to Wrangel Island?
3. What did the girls Pagnasuk and Makpii do all day?
4. How were they rescued?

Of course, it would have been wonderful if I could have gone to Alaska to see Wrangel Island, where the group waited for rescue. It would have been wonderful if I could have interviewed some of the people who had been on the expedition. I could not do either of these things.

I had to travel in my imagination. So I looked for books that would take me on this expedition. I found Captain Robert Bartlett's account of the expedition, the boat getting rammed by ice and sinking, and his long 600-mile walk to get help. I found the meteorologist William Laird McKinlay's account of the boat sinking, the time on the iceberg, the long walk to Wrangel Island, and the rescue. I read these two books many times—until I knew them as well as I would have if I had been sitting and talking with Robert Bartlett and William Laird McKinlay.

I also wanted to write about the two Iñupiaq girls and their parents who were on the expedition. Bartlett and McKinlay gave few details of this family, though the father Kurulluk's hunting was key to the survival of the group on Wrangel Island.

I had to learn details of Iñupiat life. I wished for an Iñupiaq neighbor. But I live in Iowa and do not have such a neighbor. Once again I had to travel to visit the Iñupiat in my imagination.

I searched for books by people who lived in Alaska or who visited or spent time with the Iñupiat. I found writing by Iñupiaq people. I found writing about the Iñupiat. I found a website constructed by the Iñupiaq History Language and Culture center where I could look at pictures of Iñupiaq dress and read articles about their lives.

I learned that people in the cold climate of Arctic Alaska could not survive without warm boots. There were no stores in 1913 where people could go to buy warm boots. Iñupiaq women had to sew such boots. If they made poor boots, boots that let in snow or water, feet would freeze and people would die. I found a book about sewing with skins that showed me how Iñupiaq women cut and sewed these important boots.

And eventually I found a friend in Alaska who is married to an Iñupiaq man and could add more details to my picture of Iñupiaq life.

Debby and George Edwardson. Debby Edwardson is a fellow writer and author of Whale Snow.

Writing the Story

As with writing about a person, or a place, gathering the information—doing the research—is one step, figuring out how to tell the story is another step. Once I had learned the details of the expedition and some details of Iñupiaq life I had to decide how to tell the story.

Others have written of the *Karluk* expedition, including one account with invented characters. I decided I did not want to add characters. I wanted to tell the real story of the *Karluk* expedition, as much as I knew of it.

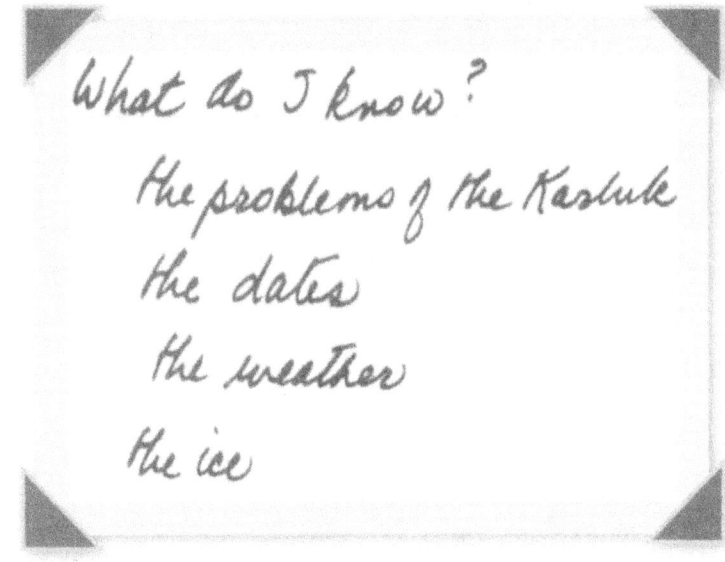

I reviewed my research and wrote about what I had learned. There are places in the story where we cannot actually know what happened. We cannot know what the young girls Pagnasuk and Makpii actually thought when the piece of ice broke through the side of their boat, or what they thought about living in the icehouse on the island of ice. When I had to speculate I was careful to tell readers that what I was writing was my guess.

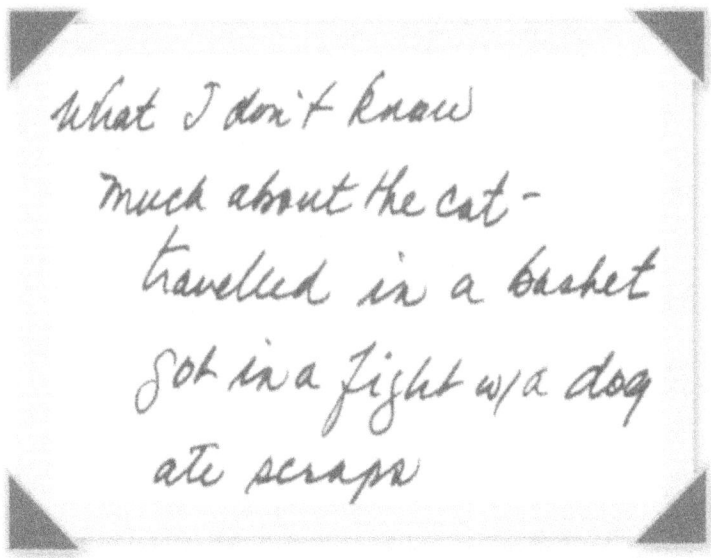

Writing a Made-up Story

A Made-up Story in a Historical Time: *Grandmother Bryant's Pocket*

One of the great pleasures for many writers is inventing characters and situations, writing the lives of made-up people. Writing made-up stories gives us another world to think about. The events in this "other world" often take place in a time different from our own time.

I have always liked thinking and wondering about what life was like in earlier times. Doing the research and writing for *Grandmother Bryant's Pocket* was a great treat for me because it gave me a chance to "live" in a different time from my own time—eighteenth-century Maine.

When I was a child, growing up on the farm in Maine, I often wondered about the many generations of my family who had lived on that farm before we did. I'd walk the fields and lanes and wish I could see what children did a hundred or two hundred years ago on those same fields. I tried to imagine what they might have done, but I had little information to help with my imaginings. The Briggs farmhouse had burned when my grandfather was a boy, so there were no old clothes, journals, or other information.

As an adult, I read a book called *A Midwife's Tale: The Life of Martha Ballard, Based on Her Diary, 1785–1812* by Laurel Thatcher Ulrich (Vintage, 1991). This book contained excerpts from a real diary kept by a healer and midwife in Maine from 1787 to 1807. Martha Ballard wrote about her life, the people she helped, the garden she planted, the work she and her children did. Here were the details I had been looking for since I was a child. I was so excited to have some of my questions answered that I decided I wanted to write a book for children about children's lives in the eighteenth century.

Of course I had to do more research. When we are writing a made-up story set in a different time period, we have to get the details of life during that time period correct. Every afternoon for several months I went to our library and read books about life in the eighteenth century. I learned that women's clothes had no pockets during that time. A woman would have one or two pockets that she tied around her waist and wore under all of her skirts. Each skirt would have a slit at the side so she could get her hand into the pocket.

This "pocket" was made for Jacqueline by a friend. On this pocket are personal images that recall her award-winning book *Snowflake Bentley* and a lupine flower—the symbol of the Lupine Award—an award Jacqueline has been given three times.

I learned that, during the eighteenth century, most people used only spoons and knives to eat their meals, but very rich people had forks to use, too.

In addition to learning details of people's lives in the eighteenth century, I had to think about what might happen in my story. A story is more than just lists of details. As I was thinking about the story I recalled some details from my own life. Many people in Maine still heated their homes with wood stoves when I was a child. Chimney fires were common. Sometimes the chimney fires became house fires. There were fires for other reasons, too. Our neighbor's barn burned down because of faulty electrical wiring. And of course I recalled how the Briggs family house had burned when my grandfather was a boy.

My mother once told me that she thought the geese on her childhood farm could smell her fear and

Goose chasing sarah in *Grandmother Bryant's Pocket*.

would chase her across the yard though they wouldn't go after her brother. I used that detail in my story.

Wonderful Surprises

I cannot trace all of the parts of the story or the characters in *Grandmother Bryant's Pocket*—or any of my stories—to a memory or a detail I learned from reading or talking with people. We do not know where all of our ideas come from. Sometimes they just surprise us as we are writing. That is one of the reasons why I love writing so much. I love those surprises. And they only happen once I start writing.

Inventing the Characters for Made-up Stories

When I write a "made-up story" like *Grandmother Bryant's Pocket*, I get to invent the characters. Sometimes characters come into a writer's head and just stand there, real as mud on your shoes. Those are fun surprises. But that doesn't always happen. Sometimes we have to invent them piece by piece. Where do we get the pieces for invented characters?

Here are some ways writers come up with characters:

- We think about people we have known, who have been important to us, and we ask outselves if there is anything about those people that we can use to describe our characters.
- We ask ourselves what our characters would love, or hate, or worry about.
- We ask ourselves what kind of secrets our characters might have.
- We try to make our characters talk. Perhaps we use a starter like "This is what I want you to know about me . . ." or "I want to tell you one thing I've learned . . .".
- We ask ourselves what our character's best friend would say about him/her.

Those questions help us begin to form characters. As we put characters into a story we learn more about them and sometimes we add aspects to their personalities. On the other hand, sometimes we realize that a character is not what we first thought and we take away a trait we have given them. Part of the fun of writing a made-up story is that we have all the power. We get to decide what our characters will be like.

Finding Story Ideas for Made-up Stories

The idea for *Grandmother Bryant's Pocket* came from my own life, my wondering. Writers often get ideas from our own lives, from the places we

Justin as a young boy—a boy who was afraid of the wind.

love, from the people who are important to us. We write sometimes about the things that worry us or worry the ones we care about. I got the idea to write *Bizzy Bones and Uncle Ezra* because Justin was afraid of the wind when he was a young boy. One day he told me he would not get out of bed because the wind would blow him away.

Many years later, when our children were grown up and Sarah and her husband, Reed, had a baby named Owen, Sarah and I decided to write *Banjo Granny's Song* because we were both interested in what a granny might do who really missed her grandson—as I did. *Banjo Granny's Song* is the story of a grandmother who puts on her thousand-mile shoes, packs up her banjo, and sets out walking to see her grandbaby.

Ideas from What We Love to Do

Writers also often decide to write about the things we love to do. I love gardening, so it was a great pleasure for me to write *The Green Truck Garden Giveaway*. Because I love gardening I also loved learning about new and better ways to grow vegetables and flowers. I wanted to share those ways with readers.

Ideas from Reading

When we are reading, writers are also collecting details for possible stories. *Washing the Willow Tree Loon* had its beginning in an article I read about a woman who always packed her suitcase and went to wash birds when there was an oil spill.

I thought *The Water Gift and the Pig of the Pig* was going to be a story about a boy who sails to sea on a schooner when he's ten years old. I had done a lot of research about life on those eighteenth-century schooners. But when I *read* about people who can find underground water with a forked stick, I knew I wanted to write a story about that boy as a grandfather who had "the water gift."

Ideas from Elevators, Buses, and Sidewalks

When writers are standing in an elevator, riding a bus, or walking a sidewalk, we are listening for details we can put in our stories. I try to write these "pop-in-your-head" ideas in my journal so I won't forget them. I have a "go-everywhere" journal in my purse. I am always waiting to be surprised by a story idea.

Owen, Jacqueline's grandson, who helped inspire *Banjo Granny's Song*.

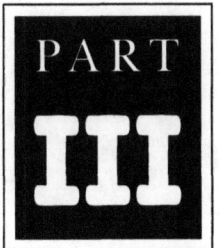

Writer's Notebook

A Writer's Notebook—For All Those Who Seek to Be a Writer

The only way to get better at writing is to do some writing. In the first section of this book I have shared some details of my writing experiences. In this section we are going to explore some kinds of writing that you might do.

Journals

Start with keeping a journal—just for yourself. As you get started on your own journal, you might want to take a look at these books in the form of journals or diaries. They may give you ideas for your own journal.

A Selected Booklist—Journaling

Books about Journaling

Graham, Paula N., ed. *Speaking of Journals: Children's Book Writers Talk about Their Diaries and Sketchbooks.* Boyds Mills Press, 1999. Though there is some repetion, this book contains excellent essays by children's book writers about the importance of their childhood journals to their current writing.

Grunwell, Erin. *The Freedom Writers' Diary.* Doubleday, 1999. An inspiring book about a high-school class of unteachable, at-risk students who are transformed by the experience of keeping diaries.

Picture Books Written in Journal Format

Axworthy, Ann, and Anni Axworthy. *Anni's Diary of France.* Charlesbridge, 2000.

Brighton, Catherine. *My Napoleon.* Millbrook Press, 1997.

Cronin, Doreen. *Diary of a Worm.* Illustrated by Harry Bliss. Joanna Cotler, 2003.

French, Jackie. *Diary of a Wombat.* Illustrated by Bruce Whately. Clarion, 2003.

Hopkinson, Deborah. *Birdie's Lighthouse.* Illustrated by Kimberly Bulcken Root. Aladdin Picture Books (paper), 2000.

Kalman, Esther. *Tchaikovsky Discovers America.* Illustrated by Rich Jacobson. Orchard (paper), 2000.

Murphy, Stuart J. *Pepper's Journal: A Kitten's First Year.* Illustrated by Marsha Winborn. HarperCollins, 2000.

Priceman, Marjorie. *My Nine Lives by Clio.* Atheneum Books, 1998.

Schlissel, Lillian. *The Way West: Journal of a Pioneer Woman by Amelia Stewart Knight.* Illustrated by Michael McCurdy. Aladdin Picture books, 1999.

Stewart, Sarah. *The Journey.* Illustrated by David Small. Farrar, Straus and Giroux, 2001.

Van Nutt, Julia. *A Cobtown Christmas: From the Diaries of Lucy Hart.* Illustrated by Robert Van Nutt. Doubleday Books, 1998.

Some Fiction and Nonfiction Books for Older Readers Written in Journal or Letter Format

Crist-Evans, Craig. *Moon over Tennessee: A Boy's Civil War Journal.* Illustrated by Bonnie Christensen. Houghton Mifflin, 1999.

Filipovic, Zlata. *Zlata's Diary: A Child's Life in Sarajevo.* Translated by Christine Pribechevich-Zoric. Penguin, 1995.

Forten, Charlotte L., Christy Steele, and Kerry Graves, eds. *A Free Black Girl before the Civil War: Diary of Charlotte Forten, 1854.* Blue Earth Books, 1999.

Hesse, Karen. *Out of the Dust.* Scholastic, 1999.

Klise, Kate M. *Letters from Camp.* Illustrated by Sarah Klise. Avon Books (paper), 2000.

Klise, Kate M. *Trial by Journal.* Illustrated by Sarah Klise. HarperCollins, 2001.

Moss, Marissa. *Rachel's Journey.* Silver Whistle Books, 2001. (Moss has several other journal-formatted titles in the series that includes this title.)

Tunnell, Michael O., and George W. Chilcoat. *The Children of Topaz: The Story of a Japanese American Internment Camp; Based on a Classroom Diary.* Holiday House, 1996.

Getting Started

Finding the Tools

Writing tools are very important. I don't want just any old notebook and a ballpoint pen that says "Beanie's Dance-a-Rama" or "Square Deal Used Cars" on it. I want a special notebook that feels like *my* notebook and a pen or pencil that fits my hand.

Sometimes I buy a notebook and decorate it

Jacqueline's decorated journal that she used to write the first drafts of *On Sand Island*.

with photos or my own drawings. When I was visiting Sand Island in the Apostle Islands, I knew I would want to keep a journal of my time there. I bought a tablet and made it special with pictures, birch bark, even scores of the gin rummy games I had with my husband.

But I also have made my own writing journals. I have made several kinds of journals. I use supplies I already have.

Making an Accordion Notebook

1. If you want to use recycled paper, find some paper 8-1/2 by 11 inches that has writing on only one side.
2. Glue or tape one sheet to another on the short edge, being sure that the writing is always on the same side.

3. Fold the long sheet of paper so the writing is on the inside. It will now be 4-1/4 inches from top to bottom. Make accordion folds about every five inches.

4. Your notebook will be 4-1/4 inches by 5 inches. Cut two pieces of cardboard from a cereal box or a cracker box and decorate them with pictures and drawings. Glue them onto the front and back of your notebook.

Making a Two-holed Notebook

1. Find some paper that is 8-1/2 by 11 inches. (Again, if you want to recycle paper you can use paper that has writing on only one side.)
2. Fold that paper in half so it is 5-1/2 by 8-1/2 inches.
3. Fold it again so it is 5-1/2 by 4-1/4. Cut where you just folded.
4. Repeat the folding and cutting with several sheets of paper.

5. Punch two holes on the end opposite the folded end, then tie a string through those holes so the pages stay together.
6. To make it mine I would decorate the front cover with tiny drawings or pictures.

Writer's Notebook **69**

Folded Mini Notebook

1. Take one sheet of 8-1/2 by 11 inch paper. Fold it the long way (hotdog style), then fold it again so that piece to make your paper 5-1/2 by 4-1/4. Open the paper up and cut on the folds. You will have four sheets of paper, 4-1/4 inches by 5-1/2 inches.

Cut along each of the folded lines to make four sheets of paper.

2. Fold those sheets in half one more time so your folded paper is 2-3/4 inches by 4-1/4 inches. Cut on the folds.

3. Stack these eight pieces of paper together. Fold in half and insert a staple or two.

This book can fit in a pants pocket, a shirt pocket, inside another notebook. It's a good place to write down reminders, things that help you remember to add an important word or topic to your larger journal.

Finding the Writing Tools

A writing tool doesn't have to be fancy. It just has to feel right to my hand. There's a certain pen that is my favorite and it's hard for me to begin writing if I don't have that exact pen. I know writers who like to write in pencil. You will find your own favorite pen or pencil.

I also like to have on hand crayons and colored pencils. There are times when our writing needs a few sketches. If I want to remember the

topsy-turvy house on the corner it's a good idea to make a little sketch of it. Or perhaps there's a funny little bug I saw on the sidewalk that I want to remember. Maybe one day I see a cloud that looks just like a rabbit and I want to remember it. You will see things you want to "save".

Don't think you have to be good at drawing to draw in your notebook. I drew rabbits in my Sand Island journal. They are wobbly rabbits with funny ears, but they help me to remember that there were rabbits just outside the door of our cabin when we stayed on Sand Island.

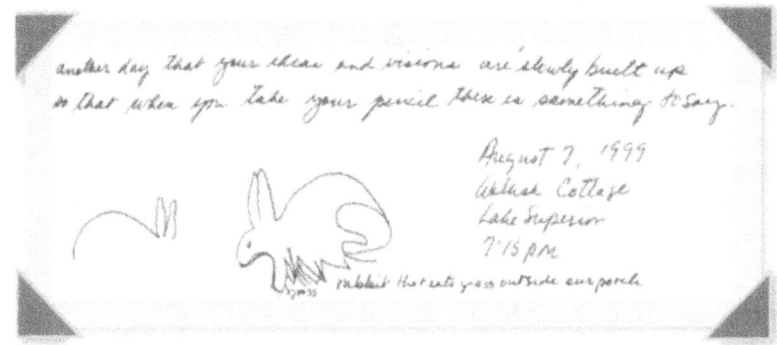

Rabbits are a part of the story of *On Sand Island*.

I also keep scissors and glue in my cupboard. Some days I want to glue a pressed leaf into my writing notebook, or a special picture I have cut from a magazine. When I was working on *The Water Gift and the Pig of the Pig*, I was glad to find pictures of schooners and put them in my notebook to make Isabel's life more real to me.

Filling Those Pages

You don't have to write long stories in your journal. There are many kinds of writing. I've mentioned earlier word lists and other kinds of lists. Here are some other ways of writing you might want to try in your journal.

1. Letters

Sometimes it's fun to write a letter to a fictional character.

Paul Bunyan has always been one of my favorite stories. I would enjoy writing a letter to Paul Bunyan or one of his cooks Hot Biscuit Slim or Cream Puff Fatty.

Dear Hot Biscuit Slim,

I know you and Cream Puff Fatty have cooked enough biscuits to fill train cars from Chicago to Duluth. But I want to know what do you do for fun? Do you make music with fiddles and dance all night long on the kitchen tables?

And what is your favorite food?

Sincerely,

Jacqueline Briggs Martin

And I could even write Hot Biscuit Slim's response:

Dear Jacqueline Briggs Martin:

I'm sorry it's taken me so long to answer your letter but these loggers do get hungry. Thousands of biscuits. Thousands of biscuits. Paul Bunyan had to move Kansas up to our backyard so I could get to the wheat fields, cut the wheat, and grind the flour. Lucky for me that baking biscuits is fun.

My biscuits are so light and good that I have to tie strings on them so they don't float away. The loggers just pull in the strings and eat the biscuits.

My favorite food is hot biscuits with north woods blueberry jam. I never had time to learn the fiddle but I can play "Clementine" with soup spoons. When I wrap a maple leaf around a comb and hum "Oh, Susannah" the birds listen so hard they fall out of trees.

Stop and have a biscuit when you are up in the north woods.

Your friend,

Hot Biscuit Slim

> **A Selected List of Books Written as Letters**
>
> These books, written as letters, might be fun for you to read as you think about making up letters for your journal.
>
> Ada, Alma Flor. *Dear Peter Rabbit.* Illustrated by Leslie Tryon. Atheneum, 1994.
>
> Ada, Alma Flor. *With Love, Little Red Hen.* Illustrated by Leslie Tryon. Atheneum, 2001.
>
> Ada, Alma Flor. *Yours Truly, Goldilocks.* Illustrated by Leslie Tryon. Atheneum, 1998.
>
> Caseley, Judith. *Dear Annie.* Harper Trophy, 1994.
>
> James, Simon. *Dear Mr. Blueberry.* Aladdin, 1996.
>
> Leedy, Loreen. *Postcards from Pluto.* Holiday House, 1996.
>
> Stewart, Sarah. *The Gardener.* Illustrated by David Small. Farrar, Straus and Giroux, 1997.
>
> Teague, Mark. *Dear Mrs. LaRue: Postcards from Obedience School.* Scholastic, 2002.
>
> Teague, Mark. *Detective LaRue: Letters from the Investigation.* Scholastic, 2004.
>
> Williams, Vera B., and Jennifer Williams. *Stringbean's Trip to the Shining Sea.* Harper Trophy, 1999.

2. Jokes and Riddles

You could use one section of your journal as a place to collect jokes and riddles. Eventually you might want to write your own jokes to add to that section. I have always loved puns—jokes involving the sound or meaning of words. I would probably have a collection of puns. Here are some examples,

> *"The baker tripped on his heel."*
>
> *"The housepainter brushed up on his skill."*

> **Pun (Noun)**
>
> A play on words, sometimes on different meanings of the same word and sometimes on the similar sense or sound of different words.

You could also try writing riddles. Riddles give clues about an object without actually naming the object. Here are some examples:

I have a tongue but cannot talk. (shoe)

I have ears but cannot hear. (cornstalk)

I have eyes but cannot see. (potato)

I have many leaves but do not have a trunk. (book)

Joke and Riddle Books

A couple of books with ideas for writing jokes and riddles are:

Brewer, Paul, and Kathleen Krull. *You Must be Joking: Lots of Cool Jokes plus 17-1/2 Tips for Remembering, Telling, and Making Up Your Own Jokes.* Cricket Books, 2003.

Lederer, Richard, and Dave Morice. *Pun and Games: Jokes, Riddles, Rhymes, Daffynitions, Tairy Fales and More* Lederer, Chicago Review Press, 1996.

---

3. Recipes

Every family has some favorite foods. You might want to include a favorite recipe in your journal. In our family, Justin made a great spaghetti sauce and Sarah had a "super" recipe for soup with peanut butter in it (I do love puns).

When Sarah and Justin were growing up we had pizza on most Friday nights. We had our own recipe for pizza crust.

Friday Night Special Pizza Crust

This recipe makes crust for one large pizza or three smalls. We made three smalls because everyone liked different toppings. We began to make pizza on Fridays because it was a way of celebrating the end of the week.

1 cup water
2 teaspoons yeast
1 tablespoon olive oil
1 teaspoon sugar
2 teaspoons salt
2 cups whole wheat flour
1/4 cup corn meal

Method:

Dissolve the yeast in 1 cup warm (but not hot) water. Add the olive oil, salt, and sugar. Add 1 cup flour and stir until smooth. Stir in enough flour more to make a stiff dough. As the dough gets stiffer, it gets harder to stir.

Turn the dough out of the bowl onto a floured surface. Knead until it's a smooth ball, about 5–10 minutes. (Knead by pushing the dough away from you with the palm of your hand, then folding it over and pushing it away from you again.)

Pour about 2 tablespoons of olive oil into a clean bowl. Put the kneaded ball of dough into the bowl. Turn the ball so the bottom (which should have olive oil on it) becomes the top. Let rise for about an hour.

Grease a 15- or 16-inch pizza pan. Put the dough on the pan and use your hands to stretch the dough and flatten it out to the edges of the pan. You may have extra dough. Trim around the pan. You can roll the pieces into bread sticks.

Let the dough rise for about a half hour. Bake at 400 degrees for 5 minutes. Then top with your favorite pizza toppings and bake at 400 degrees for 20 minutes.

Sometimes reading books with favorite foods in them gives us ideas for recipe stories.

Some Picture Books (Including a Couple of Tall Tales) about Food, Recipes to Give You Ideas for Recipe Stories

Ahvander, Ingmarie. *Pancake Dreams.* Translated by Elisabeth Kallick Dyssegaar. Farrar, Straus and Giroux, 2002.

Barrett, Judi. *Cloudy with a Chance of Meatballs.* Illustrated by Ron Barrett. Atheneum, 1982.

dePaola, Tomie. *Pancakes for Breakfast.* Harcourt, 1990.

Hopkinson, Deborah. *Fannie in the Kitchen.* Simon & Schuster, 2001.

Kahl, Virginia. *Duchess Bakes a Cake.* Purple House Press, 2002.

Lord, John Vernon, and Janet Burroway. *Giant Jam Sandwich.* Houghton Mifflin, 1975.

Priceman, Marjorie. *How to Make an Apple Pie and See the World.* Random House, 1994.

Stevens, Janet, and Susan Stevens Crummel. *Cook-a-Doodle Doo.* Harcourt, 1999.

4. How-to

Writing instructions so others can learn how to do a job or activity we enjoy is another way to have fun with writing. Think about what you love to do. Maybe you like making muffins, or playing fetch with your dog, or making art with fall leaves. What supplies do you need for this activity? What are the steps involved?

Here's an example of "How-to" writing. One of my favorite childhood pastimes was blowing soap bubbles on summer days and watching them float up to the sky. It seemed magical. Sometimes I'd make wishes on those bubbles.

How to Make Your Own Bubble Mix

a. Making the mix.

   Stir together in a bowl

   1 pint water

   2 tablespoons dishwashing liquid

   1 teaspoon of glycerine (if you have it; if you don't leave out the glycerine.)

b. Find or make objects to use as wands.

   Use a can opener to cut the bottom off a small tin can so you can blow through it.

   Cut apart the plastic rings that hold six-packs of soda.

   Bend flexible florists' wire into a shape you can blow through.

   Use a canning-jar outer ring.

   Use the ring part of the cup of a baby bottle.

c. Dip wand in bubble mixture.

   Hold out your arm.

   Turn your body in a slow circle.

   Watch your bubbles and make a wish.

d. Or hold wand up to your mouth and blow through it.

   Watch your bubbles and make a wish.

I don't spend much time with soap bubbles now. But I do love to work outside in my garden. so it was especially fun for me to write gardening how-to's in my book *The Green Truck Garden Giveaway*.

Writing the how-to for something we love to do gives us a chance to think about a favorite activity in a new way. I hope you will try this kind of writing.

5. Details

It can be fun and "good for us" as writers to look and listen for details in our everyday lives and write about these details in our journals. We can learn to notice more by practicing this careful looking and listening. Take some time to use all your senses.

Hearing. What do you hear when you sit on the front steps of the building where you live? Close your eyes and listen. Do you hear birds? Busses? Lawnmowers? Chirping insects? Kids playing? Write some of these sounds in your journal. Try adding some words to tell more about the sounds. Are they loud? Quiet? Steady, with no pauses?

Try this listening activity in other places-maybe as you are waiting for a bus, or sitting under a favorite tree, or standing on a flat rock by a beach.

Sight. What do you see when you open your eyes and look around on this same front step? You might look for colors. How many different greens do you see? Try describing one of the greens. If it is grass, does it look soft, patchy, bristly? Is it home to beetles, bugs, or ants?

What do you see that is moving? What do you see that is still? Try this looking activity in other places, too.

Smells. What do you smell on this same front step? Do you smell car exhaust? Or fresh cut grass? Do you smell cookies someone is baking in your kitchen? How do these different smells affect your feelings or "mood"? Do some smells make you glad? You can add this to your journal, too.

Feel, touch. You may not be aware of the textures of the front step of the place where you live but if you take a few minutes perhaps you'll notice that the step is rough old wood, or smooth new cement. The step may be hot from the sun, or cool from morning rain. Perhaps there's a nubbly mat by the door.

There are other textures to be aware of-a kitty's fur, a dandelion blossom, a baseball, new snow. How would you describe the feel of a kitty's fur? You might say "soft as a feather;" "a passel of tickles waiting to happen;" "a whisper." If you think about this-and other textures-you'll come up with your own words.

Training ourselves to see details and writing about them is fun. It's like giving ourselves stronger eyes and ears. And it helps us when we do longer pieces of writing.

6. What If

Books have been written in answer to "what if?" The "Doctor Dolittle" stories by Hugh Lofting are one answer to the question "what if a person could understand the language of animals?"

Bartholomew and the Oobleck by Dr. Seuss (Random House, 1949) is one answer to "what if it didn't rain raindrops, but rained something else?"

What if it actually did rain cats and dogs? Who would keep all those pets? Would someone who always wanted a dog have just the right one fall in the yard? Would someone set up a pet farm to keep them? Maybe the town grouch would get bopped on the head with a cat.

What if a barn could talk? Writer and illustrator Debby Atwell has made a wonderful book, called *Barn* (Houghton Mifflin, 2001), about a barn that tells its own story.

What if I could fly? How would the world look different? How would I get to the library? What would be the problems that go along with being the only person who could fly?

What if I woke up one morning and found a giant sitting next to my house?

I have a section in my journal and in my file cabinet called "story ideas." I know I can't finish each writing project in a day, but I want to save all my ideas for a day when I need them. The little pieces of writing that you do in your journal may be useful to you as you begin to work on longer pieces of writing.

Writing Longer Pieces: Writing about a Favorite Place

Earlier in this book I described some of my favorite places and talked about writing a story of place—*On Sand Island*.

Perhaps you have a favorite place. It might be a place you go to by yourself. It might be a neighbor's place where you know there's hot chocolate waiting. It might be under a tree in the park on the next block, or a spot by a stream. It might be a place in your own house or apartment.

Perhaps you have a favorite place where not just you, but your whole family, goes—maybe a campground, or a place big enough to throw a ball around and play catch. Maybe you go to an apple orchard and pick apples or fish in a nearby river or stream. Whatever your favorite place is, it can be a good start for writing.

Before you begin to write about your favorite place, give yourself time to think about it. You might start by making a list, as I did, of all the things you can think of that you like about your place.

You may also want to *describe* your favorite place. When we write description we think about our senses—our sense of sight, of hearing, of smell, and of touch.

- What does this favorite place look like?
- What colors do you see?

- What sounds do you hear?
- Does your favorite place have any special smell?

Think about the descriptions you may have already written in your journal. You'll want to do similar thinking and writing when you tell readers of your favorite place. Give yourself time to think of as many details as possible. It may take a while to remember the little details, such as a spider crawling up the tree in the park, or the kitty who licks your toes when you go to your neighbor's house for a cookie. All those little details are part of the place, too.

You can help yourself remember these details by making several lists.

What I can See	What I can Hear	What I can Smell
------	------	------
------	------	------

You will begin to realize that you know a lot about your favorite place. As you look at what you already know, you can ask yourself what you would like to know that you do not know. Write down what comes into your head, but give yourself time for new ideas to occur to you as you are walking to school, brushing your teeth, or helping around the house.

If your favorite place has a history—its own story—you might want to spend some time and learn about that story. There are many stories of Sand Island, and I wanted to learn them all.

If you decide to learn the story of your favorite place, there may be people in that neighborhood who remember some details. You may find some details by going to a library near the place and asking the librarian for help. The librarian may know of people you can talk with, or may show you some written resources.

Later in this book we'll discuss using your favorite place as a setting for a made-up story. Those little details may be an important part of your story.

Writing Longer Pieces: Writing about Your Hero

It can be fun to write about a person who's important or interesting to you. Give yourself time to think about the ways he/she is important to you. Ask yourself the question "What do I really like about this person?" and try to answer it.

Again, write down what you already know. Think about what you want to know and where you might find answers to some of your questions.

Learning about the Person

Before you write you will want to learn as much as you can about the person. If this is a person who has been written about in newspapers, you might want to look at some of the newspaper articles.

If this person is still living, you might want to do an interview. Interviewing helps us all learn about people and their lives. People who are being interviewed will often tell stories about their lives. If you do an interview, you'll want to have a list of questions to ask. Give yourself time to think about the questions you want to ask. You may want to know something about the person's childhood—a favorite activity, a worry. Or you may want to know details of his or her current life.

A list of questions might begin like this:

1. Where did you grow up?
2. What did you love to do when you were a child?
3. What did you worry about when you were a child?
4. Was there a person who was very important to you?

As you think about what you want to know about your chosen person, you will be able to add questions to this list.

If the person whom you want to interview lives close by, you could contact him or her by phone or letter and ask for a time when you could visit to ask some questions. If the person whom you want to interview lives far away, you could do your interview by letter, by e-mail, or by phone.

Perhaps the person you are interviewing will have letters, photos, or journals to share with you. You can read these documents with your questions in mind and look for answers. For example, what do these letters say about what the person enjoyed—what was special to him or her, or what worried this person?

Doing the Writing

Once you have gathered information about the person you've decided to write about—let's call her "Alice"—you'll be ready to begin writing.

You have some choices about how to present your information.

1. You can start at the beginning with Alice's birth and childhood, as I did with Wilson Bentley, and tell the story of Alice's life as she grew up and became an adult in the order that the events of her life happened.
2. You can choose one exciting or dramatic event from Alice's life and write about that. You will want to include details of time (year of the

event) and place (where it occurred) so readers will be able to understand what you are describing.
3. You can use what you know of Alice's life as the beginning of a fictional story, perhaps adding made-up characters or taking Alice to a fictional place, or a real place but one that she never actually traveled to.
4. You can tell the story or you can write as if you were Alice herself and let her tell her own story. That way, you get to "be" Alice.

Writing about someone important to you will give you a chance to get to know a person you care about in a new and detailed way.

Writing a Family Story

Sometimes it's fun to write about an interesting, or comical, or dramatic event that happened to our families, or someone in our families. Perhaps an aunt and uncle have a traveling puppet show and have many stories about their lives on the road. Maybe your grandma and grandpa have a polka band, or your dad had an adventure with a runaway bowling ball and chased it a mile downhill when he was ten years old, or your family went on a camping trip but left the tent at home.

Every family has stories. When you write a family story, you already know the people whom you will want to talk with to learn more details of the story.

Finding the Topic

Start by thinking about a story that always makes you smile—a story that is important to you, a story that you could hear every Sunday afternoon and still smile at the end.

Beginning to Write

Write down all you already know about that story.

1. Characters: who is important in this story?
2. Situation: what is happening? Is this story about a camping trip, a runaway bowling ball, accordion playing?
3. Details of sight, sound, taste, smell that are part of this story.
4. Details that make this story unusual.
5. Details that are especially important to you.

Writing down this information will help you come up with some questions about what you would still like to know. Try to find the answers to your questions—talk to your family members. Those answers will probably help you to think of even more information that you would like to know. You can keep asking and adding details until you think you have enough to write your story.

Shaping the Story

Writing a family story can seem a little bit like eating an elephant—a big job. There's just too much. We know so much about our families that it can be hard to figure out just what we want to write about.

It will make your writing easier if you choose one adventure or incident. If you are going to write about the camping trip when no one packed the tent, you will not need to write about all the other trips your family takes, or how long you have had the car that you were riding in when you remembered that the tent was on the kitchen floor.

As you start organizing the details of your story you will have some choices to make:

1. You can tell your story as it happened, first things first. First your family decided to take a camping trip and things you would need to take were prepared. Everyone was involved in the packing. No one was keeping track and it looked like rain, so there was quite a rush, etc.
2. You can start with the most dramatic moment in the story—in our example it would be the very minute when someone in the family realized that you had not brought the tent.
3. You can begin by describing the person most important to the story.

As you work on writing your own family story, you will be the one to decide what kind of story you want to write. You may want to write the story just the way it happened. You may want to add some made-up characters to the story. You may want to add some events to the situation. You may want to turn your family story into a tall tale. You can write your family story more than once, in more than one way. Writers often have to write a story, read it, and then decide it would be better if it were written in a different way. Writers write a lot, but we don't always write right.

Nonfiction: Finding a Nonfiction Story That Interests You

Sometimes as you are reading you will find a story that is so interesting that you will immediately want to learn more. It might be about building a real house of straw, or the Watts Towers, which immigrant Simon Rodia made using cement and bits of glass, seashells, and pieces of pottery that he collected. We all have special interests, topics that we care about, topics that we want to keep learning about. Those are "our" topics.

The Watts Towers (Los Angeles, California)

Photo credit: George Illes.

An immigrant to America, Simon Rodia, with no formal engineering education, built this complex structure of fanciful spires pieced together over a period of thirty-four years, from 1921 to 1955. He made the towers from steel reinforcing rods and wire mesh, colorfully decorated with seashells and fragments of broken dishes and bottles. In 1957 his home, which was within the collection of towers, was destroyed by fire. The city of Los Angeles thought the towers were hazardous and threatened to demolish them until an engineer's stress test proved that the structures were sound. They have now been declared a national monument.

Sometimes we have to write about a topic that is assigned to us. There are some ways we might be able to turn assigned topics into topics that are "our" topics, topics that we really want to learn about.

- You might be asked to write about your state history. At first you might think, "Oh, history. I'm not that interested." But then you walk past the old baseball field. You remember that you do love baseball. So you begin to wonder. How did that baseball field come to be in that place? Is there a story there? What is that story?

- Perhaps you are asked to write something about trees and you think, "Trees are trees. They all have roots, trunks, and leaves." Then someone tells you about the Treaty Oak in Austin, Texas and you realize that trees have stories too.

> ### The Treaty Oak (Austin, Texas)
>
> This tree, hundreds of years old, was once part of a grove of oak trees considered sacred by the Comanches and Tonkowas. Legend has it that Stephen Austin signed a treaty under the oak. When the oak was threatened by development in the 1920s, many Texans called for its safekeeping. It was added to the National Forestry Association's List of Historic Trees.
>
>
>
> *Photo credit:* Greg Leitich Smith and Cynthia Leitich Smith.
>
> In 1989, the Treaty Oak was poisoned. Its many friends tried to help. Some brought extra water. Some brought chicken soup. But the tree was dying. Then Ross Perot, Texas industrialist, donated money to pay for efforts to save the tree. About a third of the tree was saved. In 1997 the oak produced its first crop of acorns since the poison attack. Baby Treaty Oaks are now growing in Texas and other states. For more information about the Texas Treaty Oak, read *The Tree That Would Not Die*, written by Ellen Levine and illustrated by Ted Rand (Scholastic, 1995).

- Maybe you notice a grove of white birch trees at the edge of town, in the midst of another kind of tree, and you begin to wonder if someone planted them. You decide to become a tree detective and learn about that grove of birch trees.

The key to making a topic really yours is to imagine that topic as a large room (a big area of interest) with doorways to lots of smaller rooms (smaller parts of the bigger topic). Then let yourself wonder. Think about some smaller, more specific topics that you might be curious about. Give yourself time to think of some questions. You don't need to have answers—yet.

In thinking up the questions you'll begin to realize which ones you would really like to answer. Those are the questions that will lead you to your topic.

You'll know for sure you've found a good topic when you find yourself thinking about it as you walk to school, or wait in the dentist's office, or settle into your bed to fall asleep.

Doing the Research

Sometimes the topic we choose to write about is a topic we know very well. Perhaps you love horses and you have a horse. You might want to write a nonfiction piece about caring for a horse—what horses love, what horse owners have to do to keep their horses safe and healthy. You might have to do some research into various diseases of horses, but you probably already know a lot of what you will want to tell readers. Your job for this writing will be to gather together all that you know and think of the best way to share that information with others.

There will be times, though, when you need to learn more about a topic. You've decided on this topic by first thinking of a broad subject—such as birds. Then you thought of questions that you would like answered. As you try to organize your search you might begin with the kinds of questions that newspaper reporters use.

Who? What? Where? When? Why?

Perhaps one day a boy named Bill had an assignment to write about birds. He saw pelicans flying in the sky over his house and decided he wanted to know more about pelicans.

How can he make the reporter's who, what, where, when, why be useful to him?

- What are pelicans?
- Where do they come from when they fly over his head?
- Where do they go?
- When do they fly over his area?
- Why do they migrate?

What else might Bill want to know about pelicans? As he thinks about pelicans and what he wants to know he might come up with these questions:

- What do they eat?
- What are their dangers?
- Who eats them?
- Do they live in families?
- How do they raise their young?

One of my favorite parts about doing research is brainstorming the questions. It's a good idea to think of as many questions as we can, even questions that we don't know how to answer, even questions that don't have answers.

As you learn new information, you will form new questions. Those new questions and their answers will help you decide what you really want to write about. In this example Bill may decide he wants to learn about the pelicans' long trip. Or he may want to learn about other birds that have huge beaks—puffins, herons, spoonbills.

Finding Answers: Starting at Home

After Bill has listed his questions and begins to look for answers, it will be a good idea for him to start close to home. The people in Bill's community who know about the pelicans can give him details of sight, smell, sound, and touch. These people can share their excitement with Bill.

Is there a place near Bill where he can watch pelicans? What can he learn by sitting and watching?

Is there anyone in Bill's community who knows about birds? If Bill doesn't know of anyone perhaps someone he knows might know of a bird expert. He should ask around, ask his friends, people he is with everyday. A librarian at a school or public library will be able to suggest resources in the library and community. Perhaps the manager of a store that sells lots of birdseed would be able to suggest someone who knows about birds.

A Local Resource

Once Bill has found a person to talk to, he may also want to go to a place that would have information for him. Perhaps his area has a museum of natural history where he could learn about pelicans.

Perhaps your area has a local historical site, a museum, or a living-history site that will be a resource to you in learning about your nonfiction interest. If you can take your questions to that place you will likely find information that you did not even know existed. You will find the kind of information that will help you put details of sight, smell, sound, feel into your writing.

Going to the Library

A librarian in a school or public library can help a researcher find resources that might provide additional information. If pelicans fly over Bill's area every year, perhaps there have been newspaper stories about this migration that would give him good information. The librarian can also help Bill to find other resources, such as magazine articles about pelicans.

Internet

There may be some good information on the World Wide Web. There are many search engines that might help locate free public information. A school or public librarian can help patrons assess the credibility of sites that are found. Many public and school libraries also subscribe to periodical databases that allow their patrons to search many newspapers and magazines for articles about specific topics.

How Do You Know When You Know Enough? When Do We Quit Researching?

Sometimes we realize we've done enough research because we have answered all the questions that we wrote down at the beginning of our research and we have answered the questions that we thought of as we were doing the research.

Sometimes we realize we have to quit because we just can't find answers to all of our questions. It is possible that we can include in our writing what we could not learn, just as I made clear in my book *The Lamp, the Ice, and the Boat Called* Fish, when I had to guess about what someone might be thinking.

Sometimes we have to quit because we have a deadline and we have run out of time for research.

Telling the Story

Now is the time for Bill to read over what he has learned. Some information will be more interesting to him and will stay in his mind. He may read it and think, "I want to tell my Dad this," or he may want to share it with his friend. That might be a good starting place for his writing. Writing is, after all, sharing the stories we love.

When Bill sits down to write his piece on pelicans, he has more choices about how to present what he's learned.

1. He can write a factual account of what he's learned.
2. He can make up some characters to go with the facts about pelicans. When I read about people who wash oil-soaked birds, I wanted to write a story about bird washing. I did a lot of research, but when it came to the writing I didn't want to write a plain factual account. So when I wrote *Washing the Willow Tree Loon*, I used the facts I had learned and added human characters to care for the loon. Whatever Bill might decide, and whatever you decide about how to write up your research, you will want to include the details that make your story interesting to others—details of sight, sound, smell, touch.

Writing YOUR Made-up Story

We have saved the best for last. One of the great pleasures for many writers is inventing characters, situations, writing the lives of made-up people. Writing such "made-up" stories gives us a chance to think about some real situations in a new way. Writing a made-up story can give us a chance to invent another world.

Where Will You Get Ideas?

People who like to make up stories are always thinking about making up stories. There is no perfect age for coming up with writing ideas. Writers of all ages can find ideas in many places.

Ideas from Our Own Lives

We've already talked about a number of the places where writers find story ideas. Writers (including you) get ideas from their own lives, from the places they love, from the people who are important to them. They sometimes write about the things that worry them or worry the ones they care about. (Remember Justin and the wind, which became *Bizzy Bones and Uncle Ezra*.)

You may get an idea for a story from the time your family had to move to a new town and you had to leave your friends behind. Or you may want to write about a child whose dog runs away, because your dog ran away and you remember just how you felt. You can invent a character and give that character your own feelings.

Ideas from What We Love to Do

Writers also often decide to write about the things they love to do as I did for the book *The Green Truck Garden Giveaway*.

You may love to fly kites, or play basketball, ride horses, or draw pictures of cars. You might want to write a story about a character who loves to do what you do. But you can make that character a bit different from you.

Ideas from Reading

When you are reading you are also collecting details for possible stories. In your reading you may be surprised by a story idea, as I was with the article about oil-soaked birds which led to *Washing the Willow Tree Loon*.

If you read as if you were looking for entries for your journal page called "new ideas for stories," you will begin to notice that some information makes you ask "what if . . . ?" Some information stays with you and you want to think more about it. Then you know you've found an idea for a story.

Listening and Watching for Ideas

Writers are listeners and they are watchers. One of the best things a person can do who wants to be a writer is to learn to listen and learn to watch. That's another important way we gather ideas for our stories.

When writers are waiting for a bus or walking down the street they are listening for details they can put in their stories. (We can write these "pop-in-the head" ideas in our journals so we won't forget them. Remember that teeny, tiny go-everywhere journal.)

Oh No, No Ideas!

You may want to write, or be assigned the job of writing, at a time when you don't have any stories in your head trying to get out. You just don't have any stories you want to tell.

Don't be worried. There are plenty of places to look for stories.

Go to Your Journal

You can go to your journal.
Look at your list of "what ifs."

- Maybe you can start with your favorite place, put a character in your favorite place.
- Find the section on your favorite person. Put a person like your favorite person in a different place.
- Think about starting with a family story. But change the family. It doesn't have to be *your* dad who had the adventure with the runaway bowling ball. Maybe it's a storekeeper, a house painter, or a piano player.

A Real Event

You may not think you have an idea, but take a minute and think of your pets, your activities, your family's activities. Perhaps your dog ran away for five days and then came back. You know your dog really went away and really returned. You can make up what happened with your dog while he was not with you. You can make your story as realistic or as fantastical as you want. Maybe you'll write that your dog hitchhiked to Texas and back. Or maybe you'll write that your dog moved in with someone on the other side of town.

Perhaps your grandma and grandpa are coming to visit you. Maybe they really just drive, or take a plane. But you can invent a trip for them that involves roller skates, parachutes, and little red wagons.

Piggyback Stories

There are stories we all know. We can start with these stories and make them our own. Many children's books have been published that started in just this way. Perhaps you'd like to write a new version of "The Three Little Pigs." Maybe the pigs are not trying to build homes but want to drive to the ocean and they have three different cars. What kinds of problems might they have? What might the wolf do?

We all know the story of "Jack and the Beanstalk." Let's think of some changes for this story. Jack doesn't have to get bean seeds. What might happen if he traded the cow for corn seeds, or popcorn seeds? How would that change the story? Perhaps it's not a giant at the top of the beanstalk but a witch, or a good fairy. Or, maybe Jack doesn't find a giant or a witch, but he finds a family much like his own. What would happen next? Changing one piece of a story changes the whole story. It may be fun for you to write some of these variations in your own notebook.

You might want to take a character from a familiar story and put her or him in a new situation. Perhaps "Little Red Riding Hood" takes the bus to the city and gets lost. Then what happens? Maybe Paul Bunyan, the tall-tale logger, builds a boat.

Tall Tales

I have always loved tall tales. When I was a child, Paul Bunyan was one of my favorite stories. Tall tales are fun to write because we can start with a real event and stretch it. Here are some starters for tall tales. You will think of many others.

1. Perhaps you like to fish or you know someone who likes to fish. One day a fish flopped into your boat and flopped back out again. Maybe that's all that really happened. But you can stretch it. Maybe the fish talked to you while in the boat. Maybe the fish flopped into your pocket and wouldn't come out.
2. Maybe you love to play basketball. Think about what you love and stretch it. Are you really good at bouncing the ball? Perhaps you bounce the ball right up into the treetops, or over the roof of the neighbor's

house. Perhaps you bounce it up into the sky and it comes down with three birds sitting on it. When we write we get to make everything up, and we can make our stories as silly and as fantastical as we want.

3. Maybe someone in your family cooks a food that you really love, can't get enough of, could eat every day of the week. Let's stretch it. Let's say the food has some magic powers. What would you like to be able to do? Let's say the food makes you able to do that. Then what would happen? That is how we make stories. We ask ourselves "what if . . . ?" and we say, "Then what would happen?"

After You Get the Idea, What Next?

Questions

You get an idea for a story—a stuffed bear who suddenly begins to talk, a pizza that gives you the power to jump over houses—what do you do next?

Think of some questions. Let's say you want to write about the stuffed bear who suddenly begins to talk. You might begin by making a list of questions.

It's a good idea to list all the questions you can think of; but you don't have to answer all these questions to tell your story. As you think about your story, you will realize that some of the questions are more important to telling your story than others are.

Let's start with our newspaper reporter's questions—these are the questions newspaper reporters ask themselves: Why? When? Who? Where? and What?

1. **Why** does this event happen? Why does the bear begin to talk? Answering that question could be your whole story. Or you may decide you don't even want to answer that question. You just want your story to begin. "On Saturday morning Max's bear, Richmond, said his first words, 'I've never liked peanut butter.'"
2. **When** does this event happen?
3. **Who** are the characters involved?
4. **Where** does this event happen? Is the place important to your story? Is there some aspect of the place that causes something to happen in your story. For example, perhaps your story is set in a forest and it's very dark in the forest. Or perhaps your story is set in a schoolroom. Perhaps it's set in your bedroom.
5. **What happens next?** The most important question for you to ask is probably "What happens next?" How does this event change the lives of the characters in your story? That may be your whole story.

In thinking about your story you may come up with more than one answer. In the example of the talking teddy bear we might ask:

- Are there real pets in the house? How do they feel about Richmond's talking?
- Does Richmond's talking help the people in his house in some way?
- Does Richmond's talking make problems for the people in his house?
- Does Richmond say the things his owner would like to say but can't?

As you are answering these questions you will be thinking of details. You will want to put physical details in your story. You will want to tell your reader sounds, sights, feels, smells. You might write, "Our house smelled like the inside of a peanut the morning Richmond, my soft toy bear, actually started to talk. We were eating toast and peanut butter for breakfast." Or "Our mail carrier was so surprised to hear Richmond's gravelly voice he dropped the mailbag on our doorstep." Or "Owen had a toy bear he called Richmond. Richmond's soft fur was as smooth as a kitten's tummy." Details about what we can see, hear, smell, feel will help your readers imagine they are "inside" your story.

You will also want to think about the **shape** of your story. Stories are not just "then this happened, then this happened, then this happened, and then it stopped happening." Stories have a shape—a beginning, a middle, and an end.

Some Possible Story Shapes

We can all learn to be better writers by reading the wonderful stories of other writers. Reading stories will help you notice various ways that stories are shaped. Here are some of the possible shapes you will find. Thinking about these stories will help you decide how you want to shape your own story.

Stories about Problems

Many stories start with a problem or a changed situation.

- Perhaps you know the story *Corduroy* by Don Freeman (Puffin, 1976). The problem: Corduroy cannot find an owner. And he's lost a button, so it doesn't look like he will find an owner. Then a girl comes who wants to buy Corduroy but she doesn't have the money. How does the writer solve the problem?
- Let's look at *The Tub People* by Pam Conrad (Illustrated by Richard Egielski; LauraGeringer/HarperCollins, 1999).

First everything is fine with the tub family.

Then the problem—the little boy is lost down the drain.

What happens next?

How is the problem solved? Why is the problem solved?

- In *The Dirty Cowboy* by Amy Timberlake (Illustrated by Adam Rex; Farrar, Straus and Giroux, 2003), the cowboy gets so clean he smells different. His dog, which is guarding his clothes, doesn't recognize him and won't give the clothes back. How will the cowboy get his clothes back?
- In my book, *The Water Gift and the Pig of the Pig* Isabel lives with her grandfather and her grandmother. They have a pet pig, Isabel's best friend. Grandfather has the water gift. He can find underground water with a forked branch. Then the problem occurs. Grandfather thinks he's lost the water gift. Then another problem occurs—the Pig of the Pig disappears. The story cannot end until at least one, maybe both problems are solved.

We might decide Richmond's talking makes problems. Solving those problems will be the story.

When the Character Is the Problem

In some stories the situation is the problem—like the tub boy getting lost down the drain in *The Tub People*. In some stories the character is the problem. *Pinkerton Behave* by Steven Kellogg (Dial, 2002) is a good example of a story in which the character is the problem. If Pinkerton were a quiet dog there would be no story.

No David by David Shannon (Blue Sky Press, 1998) is another example of such a story. If David were a sit-on-his chair, eat-his-spinach kind of a boy there would be no story.

In *Dawdle Duckling* by Toni Buzzeo (Illustrated by Margaret Spengler; Dial, 2003) Dawdle's habit of not following is the story. If he stayed close to his mother and brother and sisters there would be no story.

Journey Problems

In my book *Banjo Granny's Song*, Granny's problem is that she wants to see her grandbaby Owen and she lives far away. She starts to walk and she has more problems—getting over the mountain, getting across the river, and getting across the desert.

In stories like *Banjo Granny's Song* the journey is really what the story is about. You might want to write a journey story. Perhaps a family takes a journey to the beach, or to the zoo, or even to the grocery story. What comes up to make the journey difficult?

Descriptive Stories

Some stories tell us about a day, or an event, or a family. There is no problem. If you have read Cynthia Rylant's book *When I Was Young in the Mountains* (Illustrated by Diane Goode; Dutton, 1982) then you know that kind of story. There is no problem. The narrator of the story is telling us of her life with her grandparents in the mountains.

- *Owl Moon* by Jane Yolen (Illustrated by John Schoenherr; Philomel, 1987) is a wonderful descriptive story. It tells us of a night of going out looking for owls.
- *Island Boy* by Barbara Cooney (Puffin, 1991) is another descriptive story. It describes the life of Matthias, a boy born on an island.

You can write this kind of story, too. You might want to write about Saturdays at your house, or another favorite day. What happens first, what happens next? What are your favorite things about that day?

We might decide Richmond only talked on that one special Saturday, and we would describe what happened on that day.

Who Is Telling the Story?

Something else you will want to think about as you write your story is the question of who is telling the story. You have several choices.

1. A narrator tells the story. Examples of this kind of story are *The Tub People, Dawdle Duckling, Island Boy*. If the narrator tells the story, the narrator can tell us everything—what will happen tomorrow, what the characters are thinking, what is going on in the next town, on the next planet. If you wrote the story about Saturdays at your house, using a narrator, it might begin "Saturday's at the Wilson house began with blueberry pancakes. Saturday was Jimmy Wilson's favorite day of the week."
2. A character in the book tells the story. Examples of this way of storytelling are *When I Was Young in the Mountains, The Water Gift and the Pig of the Pig, Owl Moon, Grandma and Me at the Flea/Los meros meros remateros* by Juan Felipe Herrera (Children's Book Press, 2002). If you wrote the Saturdays story with a character doing the telling, it might sound like this, "Saturdays at my house always begin with blueberry pancakes. My name is Jimmy Wilson and Saturdays are my favorite day of the week."

When a character tells the story, readers only know what the character knows. You, the writer, may know what is going on in the next town or what is going to happen tomorrow. But if the character telling the story doesn't know these things, then the reader can't know them either. If Jimmy Wilson doesn't know who picked the blueberries for his pancakes, then he can't tell the reader and we can't know either.

With our talking bear story we might have Richmond's owner tell the story or we could use a narrator who's not part of the story.

Once you have figured out the shape of your story and who is going to tell your story, it is time to write your story. As you write, you will get new ideas about your story. You may change some of your plans about the story so you can use these new, better ideas.

Some writers I know are fast writers and can write a story in a few days or weeks. Others, like me, are slow writers and take many months or years to write a story. There is not just one way to write a story. All writers, no matter what their age, have to find their own best way to write a story. Sometimes we are in a situation where we have to write in a hurry, for a publisher's deadline or a school assignment. Then we have no choice. When we are writing just for ourselves, we can choose to write at the pace that's best for us.

After you have written your story, put it in a drawer. You can put it under your socks in the sock drawer, on the bottom shelf of your bookshelf, or even under the hats in the closet. Put it away for a week or so. Don't even peek at it. Don't show it to anyone.

Then after a while get it out and read it. When I do this, I always find words I want to change, places where I think I can make the writing better.

That gets us to revising—the work, work, work of making our writing better.

Revising

Not every piece of writing has to be revised. Sometimes we write a story just for the fun of writing it. When the story is done, it's done. That's it. We want to go on to another story and we do.

But sometimes a story is so important to us that we want to tell it in the very best way we can. We want to tell it so well that it will be important to our readers, too. You will know which stories are that important to you.

Perhaps they are stories about an event or person or problem (whether made up or real) that is so important to us that we want to do our best writing. Perhaps they are stories that we are doing for an assignment. Then we often have to revise, rewrite to get to our best work.

Still, revising can be hard. Once we have written something we don't want to change it. We worked to get it the way it is and we don't want to do the work to change it. We want to think it can't be better. But some little voice in us often knows it can be better. Sometimes we know how to make it better. Sometimes other readers—our friends, our classmates, our editors, our teachers—suggest ways we might make the writing better.

As you are reading over your story looking for ways to make it stronger, it might be useful to keep these questions in mind.

1. Can you add details to make your characters more clear to readers? Remember to use words of our senses—sight, sound, touch, taste, smell—whenever you can.
2. Can you add action words? Make your characters *do* something that will make them more interesting to readers?
3. Is the plot, that is, what happens in the story, as clear and interesting as it can be?
4. Have you described the setting of your story with the best words you can think of?

Give yourself time to make the changes that seem important to you as you reread your manuscript with the above questions in front of you.

What Next?

Some writers think a piece of writing can never be "finished," that we can always change a word or two to make it better. But sooner or later many writers come to a place where they think they have done the best they can do, or the best that they can do in the time they have.

When you have reread and revised your work, you may be at that place.

What Will You Do with Your Writing?

The first thing that may come to your mind is to find a place to publish your writing.

We will look at publishing later in this chapter. But there are other ways to share your writing that are just as important as publishing and just as much fun.

A Reading for Friends and Family

It can be fun to share your writing by reading it to others. Some friends and I come miles from our homes once or twice a year to spend time writing and reading our work to each other. Sometimes we just want to share what we have written. Other times we ask for help with writing problems.

In my town in Iowa, writers often have a special night at the library and we invite the public to come so we can share our work. We also invite musicians and we are sure to have lots of refreshments. We always have a good time!

You may want to find a time when your family and some friends can sit down and listen to you read. You might even want to have cookies and punch and make it a special occasion.

Perhaps you are not the only one who has written something that would be fun to share. You can get several friends together, invite family members, and even make a program.

Your program might look something like this:

MOUNT VERNON WRITERS READ

April 24, 2006
John Gage Community Hall
7:00 P.M.

"My Dog Wears Boots"
James Winthrop

"Dancing in the Basement"
Janice Wilson

"Hundred-mile Jump"
Bob Blue

Refreshments
****

Of course you can have more than three on your program. But it's a good idea for your program to last not much more than an hour. It's hard for people to pay good attention after an hour of listening.

Don't worry if you are a little bit nervous. Most writers are. But once you start reading the story you care about, you'll probably get over your nervousness.

Wear your good clothes. Introduce yourself by saying, "Hello. Thanks for coming. My name is. . . . I'd like to read you my story." Read your story and then sit down so the next person can have a chance to read.

When you are done reading, you and your family and friends can share cookies, crackers and cheese, and milk or punch.

Self-publishing Your Story

Another way to share your story is to publish it yourself—for your own home bookshelf, for your parents and grandparents, or for your school library. A story you write about a family ancestor might make a great book gift for other members of your family. A story about a town monument might make a great book to present to the local historical society or to members of the community who were involved in the establishment of the community.

If you do this, you'll want to think about typing it into a word processor, maybe drawing some pictures (or asking a friend to draw some pictures) to go with the story, and making a cover for your story.

If you are not the only writer, several writers might want to self-publish a collection of stories.

Publishing Your Story in a Magazine

There are magazines that publish the work of students. Your school or public librarian can help you find periodicals that will want to publish your story or informational writing.

There is one important thing to remember if you decide to try to publish your story in one of these magazines: do not get discouraged if the magazine doesn't publish your story. Most writers have sent stories out hoping they would be published and have been disappointed when those stories have been sent back to them. The thing to do—for any writer whose story is rejected—is to start another story, a story you love just as much—maybe more—as the one that came back. We are never done writing. We always want to be better. When we are writing to say what is important to us, it is fun to try to get better.

The Room with Beautiful Windows

Good luck with your writing. I like to imagine that all those who write are sitting in a large room with many beautiful windows and lots of tables. We each have our own space. We are each doing our own work. But we are working together. Sometimes we look up and see other writers smiling because they have just thought of the right word, or they suddenly realize what they want to say next. We smile, too. Every bit of good writing helps us all.

So, welcome to this great big room with the beautiful windows. Move your table next to mine and we will work together.

For More Information about the Author and Other Resources

Articles

Contemporary Authors. A Bio-bibliographical Guide to Current Writers in Fiction, General Nonfiction, Poetry, Journalism, Drama, Motion Pictures, Television, and Other Fields. "Martin, Jacqueline Briggs." Volume 165. Gale Research, 1999.

McElmeel, Sharron L. "Jacqueline Briggs Martin." *100 Most Popular Picture Book Authors and Illustrators: Biographical Sketches and Bibliographies.* Libraries Unlimited, 2000, pages 303–09.

McElmeel, Sharron L. "Jacqueline Briggs Martin—Coconut Cream Cake." *Authors in the Kitchen: Recipes, Stories, and More.* Libraries Unlimited, 2005, pages 153–156.

Something about the Author. Facts and Pictures about Authors and Illustrators of Books for Young people. "Martin, Jacqueline Briggs." Volume 98. Gale Research, 1998. Biography contains portrait.

Websites

Internet School Library Media Center. Jacqueline Briggs Martin Teacher Resource File. (n.d.) Online: <http://falcon.jmu.edu/~ramseyil/jacquelinemartin.htm> (Accessed July 28, 2005).

Azarian, Mary. *Mary Azarian, Vermont Woodcut Artist and Book Illustration.* (n.d.) Online: <http://www.maryazarian.com> (Accessed July 28, 2005).

Gaber, Susan. *Susan Gaber.* (n.d.) Online: <http://www.susangaber.com> (Accessed July 28, 2005).

Martin, Jacqueline Briggs. *Jacqueline Briggs Martin's Home Page.* URL: http://www.jacquelinebriggsmartin.com (August 1, 2005).

Sneed, Brad. *Brad Sneed.* (2005) Online: <http://www.bradsneed.com> (Accessed July 28, 2005).

Sweet, Melissa. *Children's Book Illustrator—Melissa Sweet.* (n.d.) Online: <http://www.melissasweet.net>. (Accessed July 28, 2005).

Wingerter, Linda S. *Linda S. Wingerter.* (2005) Online: <http://www.lindawingerter.com> (Accessed July 28, 2005).

Photo Credits

Photo of Alice Briggs from the Briggs/Martin Family Album. Courtesy of Jacqueline Briggs Martin.

Photo of Hugh Briggs and his father from the Briggs/Martin Family Album. Courtesy of Jacqueline Briggs Martin.

Photos of the Briggs Family Farm from the Briggs/Martin Family Album. Courtesy of Jacqueline Briggs Martin.

Photo of Jacqueline Briggs Martin as a child from the Briggs/Martin Family Album. Courtesy of Jacqueline Briggs Martin.

Photo of Jacqueline, Laura, and Audrey from the Briggs/Martin Family Album. Courtesy of Jacqueline Briggs Martin, Laura Briggs, and Audrey Briggs.

Photo of David, Hugh, and Stephen from the Briggs/Martin Family Album. Courtesy of David Briggs, Hugh Briggs, and Stephen Briggs.

Photo of Jacqueline Briggs Martin with photo of Blanche Wisconsin by Sharron L. McElmeel. Reprinted with permission.

Cover art and interior art from *Washing the Willow Tree Loon*. Reprinted with the permission of Simon & Schuster Books for Young Readers, an imprint of Simon & Schuster Children's Publishing Division from *Washing the Willow Tree Loon* by Jacqueline Briggs Martin, illustrated by Nancy Carpenter. Text copyright © 1995 Jacqueline Briggs Martin. Illustrations copyright © 1995 Nancy Carpenter.

Cover art and interior art from *Bizzy Bones and Moosemouse* © 1986 Stella Ormai. Reprinted courtesy of Stella Ormai.

Cover art and interior art from *Bizzy Bones and Uncle Ezra* © 1984 Stella Ormai. Reprinted courtesy of HarperCollins (representing the Lothrop, Lee, & Shepard publishers).

Photo of Mary Azarian and Jacqueline Briggs Martin (at the 1999 ALA convention) by Sharron L. McElmeel. Reprinted with permission.

Cover art and interior art from *Snowflake Bentley* © 1998 Mary Azarian. Reprinted courtesy of Houghton Mifflin.

Cover art from *The Finest Horse in Town* by Jacqueline Briggs Martin, illustrated by Susan Gaber. Reprinted with permission of publisher, Purple House Press. Copyright © 2003.

Cover art and interior art from *Bizzy Bones and the Lost Quilt* © 1988 Stella Ormai. Reprinted courtesy of HarperCollins (representing the Lothrop, Lee, & Shepard publishers).

Photo of Sarah Martin Busse as a child from the Briggs/Martin Family Album. Courtesy of Jacqueline Briggs Martin.

Photo of Jacqueline Briggs Martin in rose garden by Sharron L. McElmeel. Reprinted with permission.

Photo of Jacqueline Briggs Martin at her computer by Sharron L. McElmeel. Reprinted with permission.

Photo of the whittled spider by Sharron L. McElmeel. Reprinted with permission.

Cover art and interior art from *Grandmother Bryant's Pocket* © 1996 Petra Mathers. Reprinted courtesy of Houghton Mifflin.

Cover art and interior art from *Higgins Bend Song and Dance* © 1997 Brad Sneed. Reprinted courtesy of Houghton Mifflin.

Cover art from *The Lamp, the Ice, and the Boat Called* Fish © 2001 Beth Krommes. Reprinted courtesy of Houghton Mifflin.

Photo Credits

Cover art and interior art from *On Sand Island* © 2003 David A. Johnson. Reprinted courtesy of Houghton Mifflin.

Cover art and interior art from *The Water Gift and the Pig of the Pig* © 2003 Linda S. Wingerter. Reprinted courtesy of Houghton Mifflin.

Photo of Jacqueline Briggs Martin at her writing table by Sharron L. McElmeel. Reprinted with permission.

Photos of the cabin, tree-lined bluff, and lighthouse on Sand Island. Courtesy of Jacqueline Briggs Martin.

Photo of Zilpha Prince from the Briggs/Martin Family Album. Courtesy of Norway Maine Historical Society.

Photo of Prince Dry Goods Store from the Briggs/Martin Family Album. Courtesy of Norway Maine Historical Society.

Cover art from *Secrets of Eskimo Skin Sewing* by Edna Wilder © 1998. Reprinted courtesy of University of Alaska Press.

Photo of Debby and George Edwardson, courtesy of Debby Edwardson and reprinted with permission of Debby and George Edwardson.

Photo of the pocket, books, journal in chapter 10 by Sharron L. McElmeel. Reprinted with permission.

Photo of Justin Martin, as a child, from the Briggs/Martin Family Album. Courtesy of Jacqueline Briggs Martin.

Photo of Owen Busse from the Martin/Busse Family Album. Courtesy of Sarah Martin Busse and Reed Busse.

Cover art and interior art from *Green Truck Garden Giveaway: A Neighborhood Story*. Reprinted with the permission of Simon & Schuster Books for Young Readers, an imprint of Simon & Schuster Children's Publishing Division from *Green Truck Garden Giveaway* by Jacqueline Briggs Martin, illustrated by Alec Guillman. Text copyright © 1997 Jacqueline Briggs Martin. Illustrations copyright © 1997 Alec Gillman.

Photo of Watts Tower (Los Angeles). Courtesy of George Illes.

Photo of the Treaty Oak (Austin, Texas). Courtesy of Greg Leitich Smith and Cynthia Leitich Smith.

Index

accordion notebook 67–68
Ada, Alma Flor xi
After You Get the Idea, What Next? 92
Apostle Islands 23, 40, 67
apple orchard 5, 8
apple trees 14
Arctic exploration 17
Artic Expedition 53
Articles (about the author) 101
artists 19
Atwell, Debby 78
aunts 48–50
Author and YOU, The (series) xi–xii
Author's Letter to YOU, An 29
Azarian, Mary (photo) 7, 12, 17, 19–20

Babar the Elephant (Series by Jean and Laurent De Brunhoff) 12
baking bread 8
Banjo Granny's Song 13, 23, 60, 94
Barn 78
Barrow, Alaska 53
Bartholomew and the Oobleck 78
Beginning to Write 81
Bentley, Snowflake 8. *See Also Bentley, Wilson A.*
Bentley, Wilson A. 7, 17, 44–45, 80. *See Also Bentley, Snowflake.*
birds (rescuing) 5–6
Bizzy Bones (series) 8, 13
Bizzy Bones and Moosemouse 6, 13
Bizzy Bones and the Lost Quilt 8–9, 12–13
Bizzy Bones and Uncle Ezra 7, 11, 13, 33, 60, 89
Blanche, Wisconsin (photo) 5
bluegrass music 13
boats 43
Bolton Mountain 45
Booklists
    family stories 50–51
    jokes and riddles 74
    journal format 65–66
    journaling 65
    older readers, in journal or letter format 66
    people 46–47
    place 43
    recipe stories 75
    written as letters 73
Books about Journaling 65

Books: The Best Writing Teachers 33–34
Bookshelf. *See Jacqueline Briggs Martin's Bookshelf*
Briggs, Alice (photo) 3
Briggs, Audrey (photo) 4
Briggs, David (photo) 5
Briggs, Hugh (brother), (photo) 5
Briggs, Hugh (father), (photo) 7
Briggs, Laura (photo) 4
Briggs, Stephen (photo) 5
bubble mix, how-to 76
Bunyan, Paul 71–72
Busse, Owen 60, (photo) 61
Busse, Reed 60
Busse, Sarah Martin 13, 60. *See Also Martin, Sarah.*
Button, Bucket, Sky 13–14, 23
Buzzeo, Toni xi, 94

Cajun country 14
Caldecott Award 17, 19–20
Carpenter, Nancy 12, 18, 20
characters 59, 89
Chicken Joy on Redbean Road 14, 24
Chicken Soup with Rice (Maurice Sendak) 12
Coatney, Sharon xii
coconut cream cake 43
Conrad, Pam 93
Cooney, Barbara 95
Cora (Jackie's grandmother) 3
Corduroy (Don Freeman) 93
cows 5
crayons and colored pencils 70
Cream Puff Fatty 71
Curious George 12

Dahl, Harold 42–43
Dawdle Duckling (Toni Buzzeo) 94–95
Descriptive Stories 95
Details 77–79
details, finding 57–58, 77–80
The Dirty Cowboy (Amy Timberlake) 94
Doctor Doolittle 77
Doing the Research 85
Doing the Writing 80
dry goods store 48–50

editing 11
Edwardson, Debby and George 54
eighteenth century 57

105

family stories, booklist 50–51
farm 4
feel 77
fiddle 15
Filling the Room We Call Our Imagination 33
Filling Those Pages 71
Finding Answers: Starting at Home 86
Finding Story Ideas for Made-up Stories 58–61
Finding the Tools 66–67
Finding the Topic 81
Finding the Writing Tools 70
The Finest Horse in Town 8, 14, 20, 48–50
fires 58
first book 11
fishing 16
The Five Hundred Hats of Bartholomew Cubbins 12
Folded Mini Notebook 69
For More Information about the Author and Other Resources 101
Foreward, series xi
Freeman, Don 93
Frequently Asked Questions 11–12
Friday Night Special Pizza Crust (recipe) 74–75
friendship 14

Gaber, Susan 12, 14, 20
geese 58
Getting Started 66–70
Gillman, Alec 12, 16, 21
Go to Your Journal 90
Going to the Library 87
Golden Kite Award 22
Good Times on Grandfather Mountain 5, 14–15, 20
grandchild 13
Grandma and Me at the Flea/Los meros meros remateros (Juan Felipe Herrera) 95
Grandmother Bryant's Pocket 15–16, 22, 57–61
grandmother 60
Green Truck Garden Giveaway, The 16, 21, 60, 76, 89

hearing 77, 79
heroes 44
Herrara, Juan Felipe 95
Higgins Bend Song and Dance 16
Hill, Annamae 43
Hill, Burt 43

Hot Biscuit Slim 71–72
How Do You Know When You Know Enough? When Do We Quit Researching? 87
How to Make Your Own Bubble Mix 76–77
How-to 76
Hyman, Trina Schart 24

Ideas from Elevators, Buses, and Sidewalks 61
Ideas from Our Own Lives 89
Ideas from Reading 60, 89
Ideas from What We Love to Do 60, 89
ideas, where they come from 37, 60–61, 89
illustrators 12
imagination 33–34
Internet 87
Introduction xiii
Iñupiaq people 17, 54
Iñupiat 54
Inventing the Characters for Made-up Stories 59
Iowa (Mt. Vernon) 9
Island Boy (Barbara Cooney) 95

Jacqueline Briggs Martin's Bookshelf 13–18
Jericho Historical Society 45
Johnson, David A. 12, 17, 21
Jokes and Riddles 73
jokes and riddles, booklist 74
journal 90
journal (decorating) 66
journal format, booklist 65–66
journal or letter format, for older readers, booklist 66
journal writing 42
journaling, booklist 65
Journals 65
Journey Problems 94

Karluk 17, 53
Keats, Ezra Jack 7, 12
Krommes, Beth 12, 16, 21
Kurulluk (and his family) 53

Lake Superior 42
Lamp, the Ice, and the Boat Called Fish, The 16, 22, 53–55
Learning about the Person 80
letter format, booklist 73

Letter to Hot Biscuit Slim 72
Letters 71
Levine, Ellen 84
Listening and Watching for Ideas 90
Little House (series) 9
Local Resource, A 86
Lofting, Hugh 77
Louie (Ezra Jack Keats) 12
Lupine Award 16–18

Made-up Story in a Historical Time: *Grandmother Bryant's Pocket* 57
Maine (Lewiston) 3–4
Make a Two-holed Notebook 68
making a list 31–32
Making an Accordion Notebook 67
Martin, Jacqueline Briggs (biography) 3–9, (photo) 5, 7
Martin, Justin 7, (photo) 60
Martin, Richard 6
Martin, Sarah 7, 9
Mathers, Petra 12, 15, 22
McDermott, Gerald xi
McElmeel, Sharron L. xii–xiii, 3
McKinlay, William Laird 53
Midwife's Tale: The Live of Martha Ballard Based on Her Diary (1785–1812), A 57
Miglionico, Ray 45

naïve style (illustrations) 22
No David (David Shannon) 94
Nonfiction 53–56
Nonfiction: Finding a Nonfiction Story that Interests You 82
notebook 32
notebook, making 67–69
Notes about the Artists 19–25

oak trees 14
Oh No, No Ideas!, 90
Old Washburn 15
On Sand Island 17, 21, 23, 43, 66, 71, 78
One Fish, Two Fish, Red Fish, Blue Fish 12
Orchard Mice 9
Ormai, Stella 12–13, 22–23
Owl Moon (Jane Yolen) 95

pen and ink (illustrations) 21–22
people, booklist 46–47
Picture Books Written in Journal Format 65
pies 5

Piggyback Stories 91
pizza crust (recipe) 74–75
place, booklist 43
place, favorite 39
place, writing about a favorite 39–40
pocket 57
Potato Kelly 16
Publishing Your Story in a Magazine 99
publishing 99

Questions (about getting ideas) 92
quilt making 9
quilts 5, 8

rabbits 71
Rand, Ted 84
reading (a program for family and friends) 97–98
Reading for Friends and Family, A 97
Real Event, A 90
recipe stories, booklist 75
recipes 16
Recipes 74
Redenbaugh, Vicki Jo 12, 14, 23
rescued bird 18
Research for *The Lamp, the Ice, and the Boat Called Fish* 53
research (local) 86
research 11
researching (*Snowflake Bentley*) 45, (*The Lamp, the Ice, and the Boat Called Fish*) 53–54
revising 96–97
riddles 73–74
Rodia, Simon 82–83
Room with Beautiful Windows, The 100
Root, Barry 12–13, 23
Root, Kimberly Bulcken 23
rose garden 9
Rylant, Cynthia 95

Sampling, A: Books about People 46
Sampling, A: Family Stories in Books 50
Sampling, A: Stories About Place 43
Sand Island journal (picture) 71
Sand Island 67, (map) 40, (photos) 41–43
schedule (writing) 11, 36–37
scratchboard 21–22
Selected Booklist—Journaling, A 65–66
Self-publishing Your Story 99
Seuss, Dr., 12, 78
Shannon, David 94
Shaping the Story 82

sight 77, 79
Simon, Henry 16
smells 77, 79
Sneed, Brad 12, 23–24
snow crystals 44
Snowflake Bentley 17, 19–20, 45–46
snowflakes 17
Some Fiction and Nonfiction Books for Older Readers Written in Journal or Letter Format 66
Some Picture Books (Including a Couple of Tall Tales) about Food, Recipes to Give You Ideas for Recipe Stories 75–76
Some Possible Story Shapes 93
spider (whittled) 15
Stefansson, Vilhjahnur 17, 53
Stella 48–50
stone walls 14
story telling 87
story, family 47
Sweet, Melissa 12, 14, 24

tall tale (literary) 14
Tall Tales 91
Telling the Story 87
Texas Treaty Oak 84
Timberlake, Amy 94
time to write 12
topics 84–85
touch 77
Treaty Oak tree 84
Tree That Would Not Die, The 84
Tub People, The (Pam Conrad) 93–95
two-holed notebook 68

Ulrich, Laurel Thatcher 57

Vermont 19

Washing the Willow Tree Loon 6, 18, 20, 60, 88–89
Water Gift and the Pig of the Pig, The 18, 25, 60, 71, 94–95
watercolors (illustrations) 20–22, 24
Watts Tower 82–83
Websites 101

What If? 77
What Next? 97
What to Write: Where do I Find Ideas for Writing? 37–38
What Will You Do with Your Writing 97
When I Was Young in the Mountains (Cynthia Rylant) 95
When the Character Is the Problem 94
When to Write 36–37
Where Will You Get Ideas? 89
whichdoodle 33
Who? What? Where? When? Why? 85
Why Write? 31–34
Wilder, Laura Ingalls 9
Wingerter, Linda S. 12, 24–25
Wonderful Surprises 59
woodcuts 19–20
Wrangel Island 53
Writer's Notebook 65–87
Writer's Notebook, A—For All Those Who Seek to Be a Writer 65
Writer's Path, A—from Maine to Iowa 3–10
Writing a Family Story 47, 81
Writing a Made-up Story 57–61
Writing about a Favorite Place 39–42
Writing about a Person 44
Writing about My "Hero" 44–45
Writing as Play, Writing for Fun 35–36
Writing as Work 36
Writing Longer Pieces 39–51
Writing Longer Pieces: Writing about a Favorite Place 78
Writing Longer Pieces: Writing about Your Hero 79
Writing My Family Story 47–49
Writing the Story 54–55
Writing YOUR Made-up Story 89–100
writing 8, (nonfiction) 53–55, (a made-up story) 57–61, (about people) 79–80
Writing: Work or Play? When to Write? What to Write? 35–38

Yolen, Jane 95

Zilpha 48–50

About the Authors

JACQUELINE BRIGGS MARTIN has published 14 picture books, including the 1999 Caldecott Medal winner, *Snowflake Bentley* (illustrated by Mary Azarian; Houghton Mifflin, 1998). *Grandmother Bryant's* Pocket (illustrated by Petra Mathers; Houghton Mifflin, 1996) was designated a Notable Book by the American Library Association, as was *The Lamp, the Ice, and the Boat Called* Fish (illustrated by Beth Krommes; Houghton Mifflin, 2001). Her most recent publications are *The Water Gift and the Pig of the Pig* (illustrated by Linda Wingerter; Houghton Mifflin, 2003) and *On Sand Island* (illustrated by David Johnson; Houghton Mifflin, 2003).

SHARRON L. McELMEEL is founder of McBookwords—a literacy organization, as well as an author of more than two dozen books for educators and the editor of Libraries Unlimited's *Author and YOU* series. She is an instructor of Children's and Young Adult Literature at the University of Wisconsin-Stout. She was named Iowa Reading Teacher of the Year in 1987, and in 2003 she received the Iowa Reading Association's State Literacy Award in recognition of her lifelong efforts to build literacy and literature appreciation in the community.